Struwwelpeter: Humor or Horror?

Struwwelpeter: Humor or Horror?

160 Years Later

Barbara Smith Chalou

LEXINGTON BOOKS

A division of
ROWMAN & LITTLEFIELD PUBLISHERS, INC.
Lanham • Boulder • New York • Toronto • Plymouth, UK

LEXINGTON BOOKS

A division of Rowman & Littlefield Publishers, Inc.
A wholly owned subsidary of The Rowman & Littlefield Publishing Group, Inc.
4501 Forbes Boulevard, Suite 200
Lanham, MD 20706

Estover Road
Plymouth PL6 7PY
United Kingdom

British Library Cataloguing in Publication Information Available

Library of Congress Cataloging-in-Publication Data

Chalou, Barbara Smith.
  Struwwelpeter, humor or horror? : 160 years later / Barbara Smith Chalou.
    p. cm.
  Includes bibliographical references and index.
  ISBN-13: 978-0-7391-1663-0 (cloth : alk. paper)
  ISBN-10: 0-7391-1663-0 (cloth : alk. paper)
  ISBN-13: 978-0-7391-1664-7 (pbk. : alk. paper)
  ISBN-10: 0-7391-1664-9 (pbk. : alk. paper)
  1. Hoffmann, Heinrich, 1809–1894. Struwwelpeter. I. Title.
PT2362.H45Z625 2007
831'.7—dc22   2006024510

Printed in the United States of America

∞™ The paper used in this publication meets the minimum requirements of
American National Standard for Information Sciences—Permanence of Paper for
Printed Library Materials, ANSI/NISO Z39.48-1992.

For Robert.

My pride,
my joy,
my baby boy.

Contents

	Foreword	ix
Chapter 1	Introduction	1
Chapter 2	Childhood and Children's Literature	11
Chapter 3	Violence as Entertainment	29
Chapter 4	The *Struwwelpeter* Stories	43
Chapter 5	Parodies, Spin-Offs, and Other Nineteenth Century Children's Stories	59
Chapter 6	Contemporary Children's Literature and the Absence of Didacticism	71
	Appendix: Illustrations	79
	Bibliography	93
	Index	95
	About the Author	99

Foreword

A recent upsurge in interest in the nineteenth century cautionary tales writ-ten by Dr. Heinrich Hoffmann titled, *Der Struwwelpeter*, has initiated a sec-ond wave of spin-offs, parodies, and retellings of these immensely popular stories. Following its first publication in 1844, the book became phenome-nonally successful and flew off of bookstore shelves at unprecedented rates generating imitations and spin-offs of the stories for several decades.

In recent years a renewed interest in the tales has surfaced, as evidenced by such cultural events as the junk opera *Shockheaded Peter*, performed by The Tiger Lillies, and a National Public Radio talk show devoted to *Struwwelpeter* featuring Bob Staake's new children's book of the same title. Staake's version features computer generated illustrations and irreverently humorous text that catapults the story into the twenty-first century. Another newly released but quite different version of the story titled *Fearful Stories and Vile Pictures to In-struct Good Little Folks*, published by Feral House, adds an eerie dimension of adult aberrance to these children's cautionary tales. As well, scholars have co-ordinated academic conferences dedicated solely to the analysis of *Struwwelpeter*, and while browsing the internet I even came across this anony-mous quote: "*If you watched 'The Office' last week, there was a good reference to Hienrich Hoffmann's Struwwelpeter. I vaguely remember these somehow from when I was a kid. It's like the Brothers Grimm but a lot worse.*"

So why the perpetual interest in these tales? Perhaps nostalgia can account for a portion of it, but there also seems to be a morbid fascination with the more gruesome elements of the stories. In recent decades, authors of children's literature have broken away from the didactic tradition toward a more engaging writing style that is focused on literary quality. The didactic style of Hoffmann's book, coupled with the violent content—which some have defended as being humorous—lend a particular *novel* quality to the stories that we don't see in contemporary children's literature. Hoffmann's use of gratuitous violence and heavy-handed didacticism serve to make his directive crystal clear to children: "Do Not Disobey!"

Struwwelpeter: Humor or Horror? 160 Years Later is a critical analysis of the now infamous *Struwwelpeter* stories. Scholars of children's literature have debated the appropriateness of these didactic cautionary tales for decades, which many consider shockingly cruel and frightening. While Hoffmann intended his depictions of amputated limbs and burning children to be humorous and to warn children against misbehavior, some find the punishments to be excessively violent.

As well as examining the history of child rearing practices and children's literature, this manuscript considers the sociohistoric context in which the book was written and makes comparisons to contemporary children's fare that is similarly violent, but intended to be humorous.

CHAPTER ONE

Introduction

The Popularity

The *Struwwelpeter* stories (pronounced *Strool'-vel-pay-ter*) are a collection of children's cautionary tales published in Germany in 1844 which were written and illustrated by Dr. Heinrich Hoffmann, initially under the pseudonym of Reimerich Kinderlieb. Translated into English as *Slovenly Peter* or *Shock Headed Peter*, this collection of tales is one of many children's picture books written in Germany in the late eighteenth and nineteenth centuries. The *Struwwelpeter* stories, unlike similar children's books of that era, have enjoyed immense success which was wholly unexpected as Hoffmann never intended to have them published. In the 160-plus years that they've been in print, the *Struwwelpeter* stories have been translated into several different languages. They have been parodied as *Struwwelhitler* (among others), and they have inspired a host of imitations and spin-offs including decks of cards, children's games, and posters.

The unprecedented commercial success of the *Struwwelpeter* stories, coupled with their endurance and lasting appeal have distinguished this collection of stories as perhaps one of the most significant children's books of our time. More recently, it has inspired the popular 1998 junk opera, *Shockheaded Peter*, a traveling theater production performed by The Tiger Lillies, and has been the sole dedication of a special edition of the noted journal, *The Lion and the Unicorn* (vol. 20, 2 December 1996), designated as a publication devoted to the serious, ongoing discussion of literature for children.

The *Struwwelpeter* stories have also been the topic of numerous intellectual inquiries and analyses by scholars of children's literature who strive to understand their content which some have described as sadistically cruel, and others have described as humorously entertaining. *Struwwelpeter* has long been regarded as an example of hideous Germanic cruelty toward children in its glorification of arbitrary obedience to authority. Those who interpret the tales as frightening, however, seem now to be in the minority. In fact, much of the recent literature suggests that these stories are meant to be humorous and that children who read them will understand that humor, and will naturally interpret them as such.

Nevertheless, some individuals still struggle with recognizing the humorous intent, and some have difficulty understanding why very young children would not be frightened by them; they are still interpreted by some as violent and terrifying stories. While it is understandable how these stories might be viewed as humorous, the violence is nevertheless excessively graphic and likely frightening to very young children. Of course one must recognize the existence of contemporary children's fare that is similarly violent and may be considered, by some, to be inappropriate for children. Certain cartoons, video games, and literature is unnecessarily violent, for example, yet is somehow understood to have a humorous intent.

But the Germans were not the only ones to produce frightening cautionary tales for children. Much of the nineteenth century American children's literature was just as scary and similar to *Struwwelpeter* in its didacticism and violent content. Many American writers used a form of sadistic poetic justice to punish their young protagonists who dared to misbehave. For example, Jane and Ann Taylor, who are well known for their *Twinkle Twinkle Little Star* poem, also authored stories such as *The Little Fisherman*, wherein a boy who is so cruel as to fish with hooks, is later impaled on a meat hook in his own pantry:

> But as he jump'd to reach a dish, to put the fishes in
> A large meat hook that hung close by, did catch him by the chin
> Poor Harry kick'd and call'd aloud, and screamed and cried and roar'd
> While from his wound the crimson blood in dreadful torrents pour'd. (Taylor, A. 1851)

This is poetic justice in its most menacing form. So it was not just the American stereotype of Germanic cruelty and authoritarianism that accounts for the violent content in *Struwwelpeter*, but a more universal attitude toward child rearing, one that suggests children should practice blind authority toward adults or suffer the consequence.

The Questions

Hoffmann reportedly intended these stories for his three-year-old son, Carl, as a Christmas gift after searching, unsuccessfully, for what he deemed to be an *appropriate* book for the boy. Hoffmann apparently felt that the available selection of children's books were far too sentimental, despite the tender age of his young son. Rather than subject his child to what he considered *far too sentimental*, he opted to compose several of his own stories in verse, adding pictures in color, which he titled *Der Struwwelpeter oder lustige Geschichten und drollige Bilder fur Kinder von 3–6 Jahren*—or, *Slovenly Peter or Amusing Tales and Droll Pictures for Children from 3 to 6*.

While the very title implies humor: *Amusing Stories . . . Droll Pictures . . .* the text and illustrations suggest something altogether different. Considering that Hoffman's son was merely three years old, and that the (violent and frightening) stories of subsequent editions were intended for children aged three to six, one might expect the content to mirror the author's awareness of developmentally appropriate material, meaning that the material be appealing to very young children who may not yet be able to make clear distinctions between fantasy and reality, or between humorous and serious content, and who may be terrified by the violent acts to which the characters are subject. I therefore wonder if existing circumstances justified the content. In middle class nineteenth century Germany:

> How widely did child rearing practices differ from contemporary practices?
> To what extent do cultural differences account for the book's content?
> How informed was the general population regarding stages of child development?
> Just what *was* Hoffmann thinking when he conceived the original stories?

Were his story lines inspired by the real life experiences of his young son? Perhaps his son was a thumbsucker, just as Conrad in *The Story About the Thumbsucker*. Unfortunately for Conrad though, his thumbs are severed by large steel shears. I find this violence to be inappropriate on a number of levels, and not simply because, as a society, we have a tendency to believe that exposure to violence is generally inappropriate for children. My objections are threefold and I am left wondering:

1. Why did Hoffmann, an educated practicing psychiatrist and teacher, consider thumbsucking to be a childhood "crime" so atrocious it must be stopped at any cost? While he almost certainly did not feel, in actuality,

that it was an act worthy of amputation, he nevertheless uses the threat of amputation as the deterrent.

2. How else might a parent dissuade thumbsucking, if in fact they wish to do so? Surely there existed more developmentally appropriate and humane means of behavior modification known to parents.

3. Is abrupt amputation by a stranger an appropriate and effective deterrent, or merely a terrifying quick fix?

Supposing that Hoffman's intent was to discourage or prevent his son's thumbsucking, then surely, during the course of writing this book, he would have pondered, extensively, the most effective means to that end, which leaves me doubting his intent; was it a deliberate attempt to frighten or was it merely to modify a behavior? Or, was this psychiatrist simply unaware of the unique aspects of distinct child development stages—stages that many parents are able to intuit through passive observation without benefit of formal education?

While many have posed the *horror or humor* question regarding the *Struwwelpeter* stories, few have addressed the question in the context of its targeted age group: three years, initially, and subsequently, three to six years. And it is this context, I believe, that begs the more intriguing question; is the book developmentally appropriate for the intended audience?

Whether the content is horrifying or humorous is a difficult and complex question, dependent in part upon matters of personal tastes and subject to many variables including the reader's disposition and prior experience, the manner in which it is being read *to* the child, and so on. However, whether the content is developmentally appropriate can be more clearly addressed using specific and measurable criteria such as using accepted models of noted stage developmental theorists as a lens through which to view this work. Of course, many of the noted stage development theorists published their work subsequent to the publication of *Struwwelpeter*. However, one can speculate that, regardless of individual knowledge of stage development theories, most parents have an intuitive notion of their child's personality and maturity level, and of what that child is capable of understanding. This is evidenced by commonly used phrases spoken by parents to describe their children's behavior such as *the terrible twos*, which indicates their understanding of the two-year-old being somewhat contrary in their internal conflict between autonomy and dependence. Therefore, when determining the developmental appropriateness of *Struwwelpeter*, this study places a greater emphasis on parental intuition and accepted child rearing practices than on the scientific study of child development, which was in its infancy in the early nineteenth century. It is interesting though, to compare Hoffmann's work, in hindsight, with various stages of child development and to speculate what Dr. Hoffmann's notion of child development was.

The Stories

Hoffmann's original book was hand written and illustrated in a notebook with the *Struwwelpeter* story (Slovenly Peter) at the back. Friends of Hoffmann's encouraged him to have the book published professionally and more stories were added with each subsequent edition. The first published edition of *Struwwelpeter* contained five stories in rhymed verse: 1. *The Story About Naughty Frederick*, 2. *The Story About the Black Boys*, 3. *The Story About the Wild Hunter*, 4. *The Story About the Thumbsucker*, and 5. *The Story About Soupy Casper*, plus *Slovenly Peter* at the back, as mentioned. The second edition contained two more stories: *The Very Sad Story About the Matches*, and *The Story About Fidgety Phillip*. The third edition contained *The Story About Hans Who Never Looked Where he Was Going*, and *The Story About Flying Robert*. Eventually the *Slovenly Peter* story was moved to the front of the book where it remained for each subsequent printing, and this one story became the moniker of the book, now titled *Struwwelpeter*.

Of all the fashionable children's books at that time, it was the *Struwwelpeter* stories that were most popular and each subsequent edition sold out quickly. Other titles were published exclusively for children by various authors, but none so enduring as *Struwwelpeter*. These titles include (in alphabetical order) Wilhelm Busch's *Max and Moritz* (1867), Annette von Droste-Hulshoff's *The Jews' Beech Tree* (1842), Joseph von Eichendorff's *From the Life of a Good-For-Nothing* (1826), Johann Wolfgang von Goethe's *A Fairy Tale* (1795), Jeremias Gotthelf's *The Broomaker of Rychiswyl* (1851), E. T. A. Hoffman's *The Story of the Hard Nut* (1819), Gottfried Keller's *A Little Legend of the Dance* (1872), Heinrich von Kleist's *The Beggar Woman of Locarno* (1810), Friedrich Schiller's *The Sport of Destiny* (1786), and Ludwig Tieck's *Fair Eckbert* (1796). Most of us are also familiar with the renowned *Kinder und Haus Marchen*, or *Household and Nursery Tales* in English, transcribed from the oral tradition by Wilhelm and Jacob Grimm between 1812 and 1857. *The Grimm's Fairy Tales*, *Max and Moritz*, and *Struwwelpeter* are among the most recognizable German children's stories of their time.

Cautionary Tales

The *Struwwelpeter* stories are categorized as cautionary tales that warn children against such things as disobedience, for example. By today's standards,

Heinrich Hoffmann's *Struwwelpeter* stories are considered, by some, to be horrifying depictions of child abuse, meant to frighten and intimidate children, as were many children's stories of that era. A more widely known collection of frightening children's stories are the nursery and household tales transcribed by the Brothers Grimm. "Many adults . . . find themselves hardly prepared for the graphic descriptions of murder, mutilation, cannibalism, infanticide, and incest that fill the pages of these [Grimm] bedtime stories for children" (Tatar, 1987). However, in recent years, retellings of these tales have all but eradicated the more gruesome elements of the earlier versions. Nevertheless, the tradition of cautionary tales is evident in many of the Grimms' stories and perhaps one of the best known cautionary tales is *Little Red Riding Hood*, a story that warns children, particularly little girls, against straying from the path and talking to strangers, particularly male strangers.

Like the Grimms' stories, the *Struwwelpeter* tales are frightening depictions of what can happen to children if they are disobedient. Hoffman, though, seems to take the cautionary tale to new heights of terror that exceeds anything written by the brothers Grimm. While one particular Grimms' tale warns Little Red Riding Hood not to talk to strangers lest she be eaten by a wolf, the young reader also learns that a kindly woodcutter will come along and rescue the protagonist by cutting open the belly of the wolf, thereby freeing her, unscathed and no worse for the wear. Children likely understood on some level that this scenario was wholly impossible and therefore *fantasy*, albeit frightening and didactic fantasy. Hoffman's *Struwwelpeter* stories however, depict a more literal violence, situations that *are* wholly possible in the real world. In these stories young girls burn to death and young boys have their thumbs hacked off with large steel shears, while others die of starvation, or writhe in pain from the infected wound inflicted by a dog bite.

Many of the children's stories published in this era are gruesome, and *Struwwelpeter* is no exception, often depicting the grisly consequences of poor hygiene, disobedience, and other *crimes* of childhood. The *Struwwelpeter* stories warn children, in no uncertain terms, to behave properly, or suffer the outcome. With unabashed didacticism, the author explains to his readers exactly what will happen to them if, like "Pauline," they play with matches:

> Now see! oh! see, what a dreadful thing
> The fire has caught her apron-string;
> Her apron burns, her arms, her hair;
> She burns all over, everywhere.

"Conrad," the child who is instructed to stop sucking his thumb but disobeys once his mother's back is turned, suffers an equally uncomfortable fate. As promised, the Tailor rushes in with his steely shears, cutting off Conrad's thumbs. Blood is shown spurting from his now thumbless hands in all but the first edition:

> Snip! Snip! Snip! The scissors go;
> And Conrad cries out "Oh! Oh! Oh!"
> Snip! Snap! Snip! They go so fast;
> That both his thumbs are off at last.

Like Pauline and Conrad, "Augustus" disobeys his parents' pleas and refuses to eat his soup. Like many children, Augustus is a finicky eater. He stomps his feet, screams, and even throws his spoon on the floor, but instead of being disciplined with a time-out, a stern warning, or even a slap on the wrist, Augustus meets an untimely death.

> Look at him, now the fourth day's come!
> He scarce outweighs a sugar-plum;
> He's like a little bit of thread;
> And on the fifth day he was dead.

The permanent fates of these children are sealed. Retribution is swift and irreversible.

Views on Child Development

In order to more fully understand why adults would write what are seemingly frightening and inappropriate children's stories, we must first examine the prevailing views of childhood at that particular time in history. While many parents have loved and nurtured their children throughout history, there is likewise an extensive legacy of abuses to children throughout the ages.

Many late seventeenth and early eighteenth century manuscripts refer to the theories of St. Augustine, which are based on the Christian concept that humans were conceived and born in sin, and describe children as little more than small imbecilic and savage creatures who were inherently evil. According to William Langer, Professor Emeritus at Harvard University, "the heartless treatment of children, from the practice of infanticide and abandonment through to the neglect, the rigors of swaddling, the purposeful starving, the beatings, [and] the solitary confinement is only one aspect of the cruelty of human nature" (Langer in deMause, 1974, p.i).

Childhood abuses, while still in existence today, are relegated to a small minority of dysfunctional families and no longer considered to be generally accepted practices. Changes in child rearing have been gradual, however, and are heavily influenced by recent theories and models of child development.

So has the literature written for children evolved along with our developing views of childhood and theories of child development. Didacticism has given way to well developed characters, intriguing plots, and richly described settings that engage the reader and touch the human spirit. Various genres including fantasy, poetry, and picture books have taken the place of instructional books and Biblical passages to be memorized. Numerous awards are given to meaningful contributions to literature—for diversity, illustration techniques, and more. As well, the 2003 *Bowker Annual: Library and Book Trade Almanac* projected sales of roughly 957,200,000 juvenile hard cover books and 876,300,000 juvenile paperback books in the U.S. alone (Bogart, 2003, p. 519) with the *Lemony Snicket* series, the *Harry Potter* series, and *Dr. Seuss* topping the list (Bogart, 2003, p. 596). These statistics are a far cry from the limited selection of available children's literature when Dr. Heinrich Hoffmann published *Struwwelpeter* in 1844.

Heinrich Hoffmann

Heinrich Hoffmann was born in 1809 in Frankfurt to his father, Phillip Jacob Hoffman, an architect and engineer, and to his mother, Marianne Caroline (Lausberg) Hoffmann, who died one year after his birth. As a child, Hoffmann was described as an undisciplined and frivolous child, according to existing letters written by Hoffmann's father. Perhaps Hoffmann's father, who considered the boy to be undisciplined, and having no mother to rear him, employed scare tactics to tame his child that are similar to those Hoffmann describes in the *Struwwelpeter* stories and may account for Hoffmann's own ideas regarding child rearing practices as evidenced in his book, or at the very least, be inspiration for the stories. This is conjecture at best, however. Jack Zipes writes, "Hoffmann, whose father's sadomasochistic treatment of him determined his values and behaviors, sought to rationalize the abuse he had endured" (Zipes, J., 2000). Hoffmann's father, then, may very well have influenced the decidedly violent outcomes of the *Struwwelpeter* characters. Perhaps the cruelty suffered by these characters was actually felt by Hoffmann at the hand of his father.

Hoffmann, though, was an educated man who studied medicine, went on to become a physician, and eventually a psychiatrist who described himself as *a medical man of the lunatic asylum*. Despite his background and education, it appears that he disregards his formal training and education when practicing his child rearing technique, as evidenced by his children's stories. He seems to revert to procedures that are not unlike those that his own father might have employed: using scare tactics and threats of violence to *tame unruly children*.

Hoffmann claims to have objected to the overt didacticism in the existing children's books on the market, yet he uses didacticism freely in his own book, albeit in a different manner. His lessons are not stated verbatim as separate morals at the end of a story; they are imbedded within the story, but in no uncertain terms. In the sixtieth printed edition of *Struwwelpeter*, published by Literarische Anstalt Rutten & Loening, Frankfurt A.M. (publication date unknown), there appears at the front an article by Heinrich Hoffmann titled, *How I Came to Write Struwwelpeter*, in which Hoffmann elucidates his objectives for writing these stories.

He describes the existing collection of children's books as "Long tales, stupid collections of pictures, moralizing stories, beginning and ending with admonitions like: 'The good child must be truthful' or: 'children must keep clean,' etc." (Hoffmann, c. 1844). Hoffmann was discouraged by the dismal selection of available literature for children and admits to *losing all patience* when he came upon a *folio volume* that contained pictures of every day objects, each labeled with the actual size of the object, *half, a third, or a tenth of the natural size*. Hoffmann's reaction was congruent with his learned background when he stated, "It [the child] has not and need not have an idea of the full size of a real [bench, chair, jug]. The child does not reason abstractedly" (Hoffmann, c. 1844).

Yet, the very same Hoffmann created stories of children being burned to death and having their fingers amputated, all for ignoring their parent's advice. It seems that, if the child cannot reason abstractedly, then neither will they understand that these stories are not real, but merely meant as *humorous* warnings. Hoffmann seems to contradict his own thinking here, yet he also makes some interesting observations about children and their cognitive development. He complains of parents who tell their children to behave, "or the Doctor will come with his nasty medicine," or the "chimney sweep will carry you off" (Hoffmann, c. 1844). This, he protested, made his job as a physician difficult because children would begin to squirm and cry as soon as he entered the room, as their physician, to examine them. "On such occasions a slip of paper and a pencil generally came to my assistance" (Hoffmann, c. 1844). Hoffmann cleverly used his paper and pencil to draw a picture for the child who was then distracted enough to submit to a physical examination. His pictures served to

". . . calm the little antagonist, dry his tears and allow the medical man to do his duty" (Hoffmann, c. 1844).

In this respect Hoffmann had a good understanding of the nature of the child, despite his tendency to refer to children as *it*, *antagonist*, or by the universal *he*. Nevertheless, Hoffmann was sufficiently astute in his bedside manner with children and used creative means to divert their attention while they submit to his medical examination.

He does not, however, recognize that he uses the very same method of indoctrination in his *Struwwelpeter* stories that he so vehemently objects to in his observations of other children's stories. Hoffmann objects to children being influenced by their parents to fear the doctor (or the chimney sweep), yet when Hoffmann's *Cruel Frederick* is bitten by his own dog Tray, the Doctor comes to visit Frederick in his bed and "Gave him *nasty* [italics added] physic [medicine] too." Furthermore, Hoffmann's Conrad, who sucks his thumb, is warned to stop sucking his thumb or the *great tall tailor* will come and cut his thumbs off. According to Hoffmann's own reasoning, children will learn to fear tailors as well as doctors and chimney sweeps.

Hoffmann's first two publications were a book titled *Gedichter* and a play titled *Die Mondzugler*. He also wrote poetry which often contained social and political criticism and he published a collection of these poems in 1842. None of his work, however, was ever as popular as his *Struwwelpeter* stories, for which he is most well known. Hoffmann died on September 20, 1894.

CHAPTER TWO

Childhood and Children's Literature

The history of childhood is a nightmare from which we have only re-cently begun to awaken.—deMause, 1974, p. 1

Contemporary Children's Literature

It is unclear whether the notion of childhood, as a separate existence from adulthood, was wholly unknown in past centuries, or merely ignored. Those who dispute that a distinct developmental stage called childhood was dis-covered only in recent centuries base much of their argument on the analy-sis of famous works of art wherein children are depicted as little more than miniature adults. This ambiguous evidence is easily debated. After all, many things were missing from medieval art. With a sole focus on religious themes, virtually all of secular life was missing, making it difficult to single out the concept of childhood as a noteworthy absence.

However, it is clearly documented that children were considered, in the past, to be evil beings in need of taming and that child rearing practices re-flected that misconception in its extremes of cruelty and abuse. While it is understood that there were likely medieval parents who doted on and pro-tected their children, as well as contemporary parents who still believe that children are conceived of and born in sin (inherently evil), and some who even abuse their children, the ideas represented here are indicative of the be-liefs and practices of the majority and suggest trends in child rearing, not ab-solutes.

Fortunately child rearing practices have improved dramatically since ancient times, but it was not so long ago that, because of ignorance, children were misinterpreted as bothersome nuisances at best, and their behavior cognate to devil possession at worst. Throughout history the commonplace use of swaddling bands—the act of binding children tightly to their chairs to prevent them from crawling like animals—is now considered horrifying, as is the past practice of taking children to view rotting corpses in order that they might be more obedient.

John Cleverley and D. C. Phillips write in their book, titled *Visions of Childhood: Influential Models from Locke to Spock*, "Conceptions of children have changed during the course of history. Indeed, the views we have at present may all have developed relatively recently" (Cleverley & Phillips, 1986, p. 9). Cleverley and Phillips further note that these conceptions are ever evolving and thus our present views are unlikely to endure.

In fact, child rearing practices are typically modified as rapidly as one generation to the next. Consider the ever blurring distinction between children and adults in popular culture—tastes in movies, leisure activities, and clothing, for example. Even the most recent fashions can be easily found in infant-sized clothing. While it may seem that dressing children in adult-like fashion is a throwback to the days when children were perhaps viewed as miniature adults, our conceptions of childhood have evolved considerably. Just as we cannot judge present day child rearing practices on outward appearances alone—how children are dressed, for example—neither can we make such general assumptions about past child rearing practices based on outward appearances alone.

> The concept of childhood shifts constantly from period to period, place to place, culture to culture—perhaps even from child to child. The literature designed for childhood is going, therefore, to reflect this variety too. It takes a considerable mental leap to remember that the innocent schoolgirl intrigues of Angela Brazil or Enid Blyton in the 1940s were designed for the same age group as the sexually active and angst-ridden teenagers of Judy Blume in the 1970s (Hunt, 2001, p. IX).

As our knowledge base of child development expands, so does the literature for children reflect that knowledge. By the twenty-first century, Judy Blume's "sexually active and angst-ridden teenagers" may seem mild in comparison to some of the more recent young adult literature, such as Francesca Block's *Weetzie Bat* series, for example, but certainly were a far cry from the teenagers depicted by Blyton in the 1940s and by Brazil in the 1920s and

'30s. One can easily correlate the tone and content of a particular children's book with the prevailing political climate as well as the popular views of childhood at any given time.

Enid Blyton wrote over six hundred children's books and young adult novels during her forty-year writing career. Perhaps the best known of her young adult series are *The Famous Five* books which depict the adventures of five teenagers in an idyllic rural English landscape. These books are reminiscent of the highly romanticized American series, *The Boxcar Children* written by Gertrude Chandler Warner, also published in the 1940s. While Enid Blyton and Gerturde Chandler focused exclusively on and professed values such as comradeship and honesty (WWII era), the Judy Blume teens of the 1970s were dealing with the more immediate and personally meaningful issues of coming of age—menstruation and dating, for example—within the larger context of examining the core values of friendship and honesty. By the 1990s, Francesca Block has her teen characters dealing with all of the above, plus current issues such as AIDS and homosexuality. Blyton's teens were sheltered and exuded a romanticized innocence which Blume's characters, and even more so, Block's characters, appropriately shed. A typical passage from Blyton's work reads:

> Anne saw some cows pulling at the grass in a meadow as they passed. "It must be awful to be a cow and eat nothing but tasteless grass," she called to George. "Think what a cow misses—never tastes an egg and lettuce sandwich, never eats a chocolate eclair, never has a boiled egg—and can't even drink a glass of ginger-beer! Poor cows!" (from *Five Get Into Trouble*, 1949)

. . . as opposed to a typical passage from Blume's work which reads:

> "*Guess Who?*" Janie asked. "How do you play that?" Norman explained. "See, I turn off all the lights and the boys line up on one side and the girls on the other and then when I yell GO the boys run to the girls' side and try to guess who's who by the way they feel." . . . "Forget it," Gretchen said and we all agreed. Especially me—I kept thinking of those six cotton balls. They weren't so far below my neck. "Okay," Norman said. "We'll start with *Spin the Bottle*." (Blume, 1970)

Blume's (female) characters concern themselves with coming of age by focusing inward, on their sexuality and on how others relate to them: Do boys like me? Do they think I'm attractive? While Blyton's characters are focused outward, on exploring the world around them and considering how they fit into the adult world of responsibility. Both sets of characters are clean-cut and relatively happy teenagers, Blume just presents a less romanticized version of the teenager.

Angela Brazil also presented more realistic characters: girls who were active, robust, and spirited. Her characters might have been silly, vain, or selfish, but could just as easily have been reliable, honest, and well-intentioned. Whatever their characteristics, they coexisted to each other's mutual benefit and managed to learn from each other's mistakes. This was a rare departure from the instructional and didactic books of that time period for children and young adults.

So, in order to understand more fully the evolution of children's literature, we must consider the established view, by adults, of childhood at any given time in history.

Childhood Through the Ages

According to Philippe Aries, in his famous yet often disputed work titled *Centuries of Childhood*, the concept of the "Ages of Life" originated in the sixth century and there are countless medieval texts on this same theme. One such text titled, *Le Grande Proprietyaire de toutes choses*, identifies seven ages which correspond with the seven planets. They are: Childhood, Pueritia, Adolescence, Youth, Senectitude, Old Age, and Senies. Childhood is the age when "the teeth are just planted" (not yet visable) and therefore, the person cannot yet speak. Pueritia is so named because "the person is still like the pupil in the eye." Adolescence spans the chronological ages of fourteen until twenty-eight, because "the person is big enough to bear children." After adolescence comes Youth, a time when "the person is in his greatest strength." Next comes Senectitude, at about the age of forty-five, when "the person is grave in his habits and bearing." During Old Age "the person has not such good sense as they had" and finally, Senies, which is the second stage of old age when "the old man is always coughing, spitting, and dirtying" (Aries).

Although Aries acknowledges these developmental stages, he holds fast to the notion that *childhood* was virtually unknown until recent centuries. However, despite the distinct labels for the various stages in this theory of human development, childhood, as we know it today, was quite different back in the sixth century. These stages seem to connote more of an observed biological change in appearance, than they do any perceived psychological, emotional, or cognitive differences. For example, Aries documents the behavior of adults in front of their children as being no different than if the children were not present. Sexual activity, for example, was not necessarily curtailed just because there were children in the room.

One of the unwritten laws of contemporary morality, the strictest and best respected of all, requires adults to avoid any reference, above all any humorous reference, to sexual matters in the presence of children. This notion was entirely foreign to the society of old. The modern reader of the diary in which Henri IV's physician, Heroard, recorded the details of the young Louis XIII's life is astonished by the liberties which people took with children, by the coarseness of the jokes they made, and by the indecency of gestures made in public which shocked nobody and which were regarded as perfectly natural. (Aries, 1962, p. 100)

Aries asserts that childhood is a modern concept, although some disagree. He contends that a separate and distinct stage of human development called *childhood* was all but nonexistent in the Medieval period. It appeared, he states, in the upper classes in the sixteenth and seventeenth centuries, solidified itself somewhat more fully in the eighteenth century upper classes, and was eventually widely recognized in the twentieth century by both the upper and lower classes. Childhood, according to Aries, did not really penetrate the great masses of the lower and lower-middle classes until the late nineteenth and early twentieth centuries.

In this new moral climate [1671] a whole pedagogic literature for children as distinct from books for adults made its appearance. It is extremely difficult, with the countless manuals of etiquette produced from the sixteenth century on, to distinguish between those intended for adults and those intended for children. This ambiguity is due to factors connected with the structure of the family and the relationship between the family and society, which are examined in the last part of this study. (Aries, 1962, p. 121)

Aries, and those scholars who agree that a separate concept of childhood was virtually unknown in the Middle Ages, base their findings primarily on artists' portrayals of children in their portraits. Other evidence was drawn from literature, personal diaries, inscriptions on family tombs, and from toys and clothing of that era. It is the artist's work however, that is most often cited as the basis for the belief in the notion that childhood was altogether unknown. Children were depicted as miniature adults dressed in adult clothing, with adult facial features, and rendered in adult poses. This evidence however, that of the artist's portrait, is considered imprecise by many.

Lloyd deMause, who wrote *The History of Childhood*, would argue that artists of that era were highly skilled, as evidenced by the remainder of their works—that part of the portrait which did not include children as subject matter, and that the depiction of children as miniature adults was intentional, a deliberate attempt to ignore childhood and children, who were considered evil. This reasoning coincides with George Payne's examination, in his work titled *The Child in Human Progess*, of the vast extent of infanticide and brutality toward children in the past. According to deMause, the further back in history one goes, the lower the level of child care, and the more likely children are to be killed, abandoned, beaten, terrorized, and sexually abused (deMause, 1974, p. 1).

Infanticide was an acceptable practice in ancient times. It was a common occurence, for example, to expose children to the elements, particularly girls, so that they might die. Girls were undervalued, as evidenced by the instructions of Hilarion, who lived in the third century AD, to his wife Alis: "If you give birth to a boy let it live; if it is a girl, expose it" (deMause, 1974, p. 27). The children most at risk for infanticide were females, illegitimate children, and those children born with birth defects. "Children were thrown into rivers, flung into dung heaps and cess trenches, potted in jars to starve to death, and exposed on every hill and roadside, a prey for birds, food for wild beasts to rend" (deMause, 1974, p. 25). Children who cried too little or too much, were not perfect in shape or size, or were otherwise flawed, were generally killed, even in wealthy families.

In the second century AD, a physician by the name of Soranus of Epheuss wrote *How to Recognize the Newborn That is Worth Rearing*, which was an assessment of the child's overall health. The very title clearly suggests the assumption that not every child was worth rearing. Only the lives of those who met certain criteria would be spared, and Soranus generously assists parents in their decision making process—to spare or to murder their offspring—with his how-to manual. The work, which in some ways resembles today's Apgar score—the five signs observed and noted after birth (heart rate, respiratory rate, reflex irritability, muscle tone, and color)—but had an altogether different purpose, helped parents to decide whether to raise the child, or to expose (kill) it. Typically, female children and children with any perceived defect were exposed and healthy male children were retained.

The stoic Roman philosopher, Seneca, who lived from 3 BC until 65 AD wrote, "Mad dogs we knock on the head; the fierce and savage ox we slay; sickly sheep we put to the knife to keep them from infecting the flock; unnatural progeny we destroy; we drown even children who at birth are weakly and abnormal" (Basore, 1963, p. 145). According to deMause, child sacrifice was practiced by the Irish Celts, the Gauls, the Scandanavians, the Egyptians, the Phoenecians, the Moabites, the Ammonites, and the Israelites. "Thousands of bones of sacrificed children have been dug up by archaeologists, reaching back to the Jericho of 7,000 BC" (deMause, 1974, p. 27). DeMause continues to say that sealing children in walls, bridges, and foundations of buildings was an accepted means of strengthening the structure.

Furthermore, children who survived infanticide and dangerously improper care—corsetting, tossing, shaking, violent rocking, freezing, burning, or exposure—were routinely sold. The sale of children was legal in Babylonia and perhaps elsewhere. In the twelfth century the English sold their children to the Irish as slaves, and in Russia the sale of children was not outlawed until the nineteenth century. Up until the early eighteenth century, the average child of wealthy parents spent their early years in the home of a wet nurse and was later sent out to apprenticeship or school, spending very little, if any time with their birth parents. Children under the care of a wet nurse, usually a peasant woman whose husband was paid a monthly fee for his wife's services, had a marginal chance of survival as little or no supervision by the child's birth parents occurred. Many children were sent out on the day of their birth, their fate dependent on many variables—duration of the stay, physical and emotional health of the wet nurse, stability of her home, and so on. Factors including the Black Plague, smothering, and pregnancy were frequently occurring events that caused the child to die or to be sent home to the birth parents.

Formal Education

The seventeenth and eighteenth century Puritans also believed people to be inherently sinful and their child rearing practices were designed to break the child's willful nature in order to spare the child's soul. Self-will, they believed, was at the heart of all sin and misery in the world. John Wesley, who founded the Methodist movement wrote, "If you spare the rod, you spoil the child; if you do not conquer, you ruin him" (Cleverley & Phillips). Wesley believed that education was necessary to cure man of all of the "spiritual diseases, which everyone that is born of woman, brings with him into the world" (Cleverley & Phillips). By breaking the will of the child, he believed he could combat pride, self-worship, atheism, love of the world, anger, and other evils. Children, he thought, must be raised to fear God and had to be prevented from gratifying their senses. Wesley's schools were rigidly prescriptive. "The girls were to rise at 4 AM—winter and summer—and spend an hour in religious exercise followed by a period of reflection and self-examination. At five they attended public worship then worked at their books until breakfast" (Cleverley & Phillips, 1986, p. 30). The school day ended at 5 PM. Additional school work, prayer, and exercise followed the evening meal, and no time at all was allotted for play . . . or for gratifying the senses.

Not all educators ascribed to these beliefs, however, and gradually, the notion of children being inherently evil began to change. A major influence on this shifting paradigm was John Locke, the English academic who lived from 1632 until 1741. Locke published *Some Thoughts Concerning Education* in 1693 and believed that man [sic] was not born with universally innate knowledge, as was widely believed, but that knowledge was a result of postnatal education, or experience in the form of both sensation and reflection. These revolutionary ideas flew in the face of the notion that man is inherently evil. Locke's work, which was widely accepted, posits the notion that environmental influences have a much more dramatic impact on human behavior than does heredity in determining whether a person is good or evil.

Following Locke's work, the possibilities inherent in education were being widely affirmed. "In the course of the next two hundred years, various schemes of sensory training were devised" (Cleverley & Phillips, 1986, p. 21), such as Maria Montessori's sense exercises and Johann Pestazolli's object lessons. Considered a major breakthrough in teaching, we still employ similar experiential teaching techniques today.

While much of the harsh Puritanical practices of child rearing have disappeared, they have not succumbed altogether. The relatively recent 1976 publication titled *Family Life* states that "all children—not just certain children, all children—are born delinquent" (Stedman, 1976, p. 83). These views however, are typically held by a minority of fundamentalist religious groups and not shared by the mainstream.

The Swiss philosopher Jean-Jacques Rousseau (1712–1778) contended that children were essentially good and that the advent of all evil behavior can be traced to an outside environmental source. Rousseau's writing was contradictory at times, however, as he is also known to have said that evil is mankind's own creation. Nevertheless, Rousseau rejected the notion that man is inherently evil, having been born of a woman—in sin.

Rousseau's thinking was a radical departure from past thought and some contemporary educators took his ideas to the opposite extreme. Rather than attempting to break the child's will, A. S. Neill for example, headmaster at the famous Summerhill School, strove to nurture the free will of the child. Educators today still disagree on which is the preferred disciplinary model—freedom or restraint—and the overall focus of childhood and children's education has shifted, giving momentum to the child study movement. Few people, however, still concern themselves with the question of whether children are inherently good or inherently evil; rather they seek to understand how children develop cognitively, socially, emotionally, psychologically, and physically.

Early Children's Books

Children's literature is a relatively recent creation when we consider *literature* to be those fictional stories which have a distinct focus on intriguing plots, well developed and believable characters, richly described settings, and relevant themes, as well as a particular style and point of view. Prior to the 1866 publication of Lewis Carroll's landmark *Alice in Wonderland*, a fantasy which is noted for its complete absence of didacticism, most Western children's books were limited to instructional manuals, Bible passages, moral fables, or cautionary tales. These heavy-handed didactic tales reflected the values that society held dear, but also society's perceptions of child rearing and child development.

Unlike early didactic tales, well written children's literature recognizes and appeals to the reader's intelligence and allows the reader to draw their own conclusions based on the reader's prior experiences and background knowledge. This is known as the *Reader Response* approach to literary criticism, and is considered a much more powerful way of conveying information than simply *telling* the reader what to think. As an example, we can contrast the didactic message in the Charles Perrault version of *Little Red Riding Hood*, or *Petit Chaperone Rouge* in French, with a contemporary version published in 1997 by Susan Lowell titled *Little Red Cowboy Hat*.

In the Perrault version, published in his 1697 collection titled *Contes ou contes temps passe'*, or *Stories of Past Times*, he explicitly spells out the moral for the reader:

> From this story one learns that children
> Especially young lasses
> Pretty, courteous and well-bred
> Do very wrong to listen to strangers

The lesson is explicitly stated for the reader who needn't infer anything.

By contrast, Susan Lowell's version allows the reader to glean their own meaning from the text. They can determine the lesson based on evidence supplied in the story—specifically, the character's actions and words. Lowell's main character, Little Red Cowboy Hat, is an assertive and capable young girl who sets off on horseback for her grandmother's house, stopping en route to talk to the wolf. The wolf, of course, precedes her to grandmother's house and attempts to devour her but fails when the grandmother returns home unexpectedly. Together Little Red Cowboy Hat and her grandmother chase off the wolf. Never does the author tell the reader what to think. Instead, readers will infer for themselves what is safe or appropriate behavior. Didactic tales do not recognize the reader's intelligence or ability to make such determinations, nor do these tales allow for the child to think critically.

Before written stories, there were oral stories told in the evenings after a hard day's labor, with little distinction between stories told for children and stories told for adults. There were just stories, usually about everyday life, but often containing witches, magical spells, or other fantastic elements. Many of these oral peasant tales were collected and published, such as the folk and fairy tales collected and transcribed by Jacob and Wilhelm Grimm.

The earliest printed books were hand written and illustrated Bible passages targeted primarily at the wealthy upper classes. Intended as instructional manuals, they were often written in easy to memorize rhymed couplets or as lengthy and tedious dialogue between teacher and student. One well known manuscript of this type, the *Biblia Pauperum*, or *Bible of the Poor*, printed in the fourteenth century, is a collection of graphic scenes from the Old and New Testaments, and served as a model for subsequent printed block books of the fourteenth and fifteenth centuries.

It was not until Johannes Gutenberg invented his moveable-type press in 1436 that printed books became affordable and therefore available to the masses, despite the Chinese invention of moveable type hundreds of years earlier. As others learned the printing trade, more and more books became available to the public. Among the first books to be mass produced in this manner were *Aesop's Fables* printed in 1484 in England.

The *Hornbook* for children was popular from the 1500s until the 1700s and appeared in various forms. Typically, the Hornbook was printed matter—ABCs, Bible passages, or morals—affixed to a wooden paddle and covered in a thin layer of transparent animal horn to protect the valuable paper below. Later Hornbooks were crafted from metal, leather, and ivory. A hole in the book's handle allowed children to carry the book around the neck and the paddle shape often doubled as a racquet on the playground. The durable hornbook was revolutionary because children could now hold their own book in their own hands and read it up close, as opposed to reading from a precious manuscript that was held at a distance by the teacher, initiating the vital interaction between reader and text that is described in the Reader Response method of literary criticism.

The Hornbook and other books published at this time, such as *Spiritual Milk for Boston Babes in Either England* by John Cotton (1585–1652), published in England in 1646, were strictly Puritanical. However, by the eighteenth century chapbooks had gained in popularity and were widely read by both children and adults. These small, inexpensive, crude paper books were sold by peddlers, or *chapmen*, and contained tales of adventure, crime, and romance as well as fairy tales and riddles. By now, there existed a small body of literature that held great appeal for children: Perrault's collection of fairy tales titled *Histoires ou contes du temps passe'* was published in France in 1679, the Persian, Arabian, and Indian folktale collection titled *Arabian Nights* was translated into English and published in 1706, Daniel Defoe's *The Life and Strange and Surprising Adventures of Robinson Crusoe* was published in 1719, and in 1726 Jonathan Swift's *Gulliver's Travels* was published. While these stories were not intended exclusively for an audience of children, children greatly enjoyed reading these tales of adventure.

Noting the growing popularity of books among children, John Newbery published *A Little Pretty Pocket-Book* in 1744. While the primary function of the book was to teach the alphabet, it also contained deliberate humor and openly set out to amuse and entertain children. This was a dramatic break from the Puritanical printed matter intended for children and now writers began to produce a new variety of children's book, one that infused entertaining story telling with the pedagogical focus on learning, and was meant to influence the moral development of children: the *didactic tales*.

Didacticism endured into the next century and, in fact, still appears in children's books today, although less frequently. These stories, which were usually conversational in format, contained lengthy narratives between adult and child that set out to teach specific moral lessons. Children were made to wade through pages of moral platitude and preaching to get to even a hint of adventure or humor.

By the nineteenth century Jacob and Wilhelm Grimm had produced a collection of fairy tales in their *Kinder und Haus Marchen*, or *Nursery and Household Tales*, many of which are still popular today, and Washington Irving produced the folktales titled *Rip Van Winkle* and *The Legend of Sleepy Hollow*. These folk and fairy tales were also meant to teach a lesson or a moral. However, by 1868, Louisa May Alcott had published *Little Women*, complete with well-rounded and believable characters who experienced life's trials and tribulations in a realistic manner that appealed to the intelligent reader. In 1872 Charles Dodgson published his high fantasy children's adventure titled *Alice's Adventures in Wonderland*, under the pen name Lewis Carroll, which was produced purely for the entertainment and enjoyment of children, making it a landmark publication. However, not all authors of children's literature were producing stories intended for the pure enjoyment of children. Cautionary tales, moralistic fables, and didacticism were still popular, although rapidly becoming less so than in previous decades.

Childhood and Children's Literature

Just as the Puritans believed children to be inherently evil, and addressed their concerns, in part, by producing Bible scripture for children to read, contemporary authors of children's literature craft their writing according to present day perceptions of children as fragile yet intelligent beings in need of nurturing and protection. As we follow children's "literature" through the ages we see a gradual shift away from didacticism, to a more engaging style of writing that is congruent with society's current views of children. The vast majority of contemporary publishers of fictional children's literature are looking for books to delight and entertain, and for books in which the lesson, if present at all, is imbedded in the intriguing plot and the believable characterization rather than overtly stated in a didactic manner. The fact that earlier children's books were not so entertaining is a reflection not only of society's perceptions of children (as evil beings in need of taming) but also of our lack of understanding of how children learn.

While adults have always been aware of the child's physical development, for that can be easily and passively observed, the child's emotional and cognitive development are not so easily observed. In recent centuries, the work of noted developmental theorists such as Jean Piaget (1896–1980) and Lev Vygotsky (1896–1934) have helped us to understand the unique ways that children develop cognitively. Piaget's work suggests that cognition develops in four distinct stages which he named: the Sensorimotor stage, the Preoperational stage, the Concrete Operational stage, and the Formal Operations stage. According to Piaget children move from stage to stage, or from birth to adulthood, according to four interrelated factors: maturation, experience, social interaction, and equilibration. *Maturation* refers to the physical and psychological growth of the child. *Experience* refers to interaction between the child and their environment, and *Social Interaction* refers to the child's interactions with others. Lastly, *Equilibration* occurs when the child brings together maturation, experience, and social interaction to build mental schema.

Vygotsky's theory of child development was more of a continuum, rather than something that could fit neatly into discrete stages and his work emphasized the roles of historical, cultural, and social factors on the child's cognitive development. In 1956, psychologist Erik Erikson developed yet another stage development theory. He defined eight stages of social and emotional development:

1. Basic Trust v. Basic Mistrust,
2. Autonomy v. Shame,

3. Initiative v. Guilt,
4. Industry v. Inferiority,
5. Identity v. Identity Diffusion,
6. Intimacy v. Isolation,
7. Generativity v. Self-Absorption, and
8. Integrity v. Despair.

So, with our developing awareness of childhood and cognitive development, contemporary authors, illustrators, and publishers of children's literature now design children's books in conjunction with this knowledge. Children no longer suffer the didactic sermons intended to teach them life's lessons. Nor are they turned away by condescending language that over explains concepts and ignores the child's intelligence. As well, the unnaturally controlled vocabulary, as in the early Basal Readers, has all but disappeared from library shelves.

A children's book can now be judged on the same literary standards used to judge any book. Typically, they are: plot, characterization, setting, theme, style, and point of view. Children are attracted to books that are personally satisfying to read and aesthetically pleasing to behold. Children can be taught to comprehend vocabulary that is beyond their reading level by using any number of comprehension strategies. This cognitive exercise leads to increased language skills and knowledge. The child's developmental stage is considered even in the physical design and layout of a book. Books for infants are typically constructed of quilt-like soft fabric pages, while the books for toddlers and preschoolers might be made from more durable materials such as cardboard (board books) that can better withstand constant chewing, throwing, or dropping. By elementary school most children are able to understand that we treat books with respect and can handle the thirty-two page picture book format. Likewise, upper elementary school children prefer chapter books and by middle and high school they are reading young adult novels containing few, if any, illustrations.

In Heinrich Hoffmann's *Struwwelpeter*, we find an intriguing mix of traditional elements with some stylistic elements that might have been considered avant garde for its time, certain components that were dramatically different than anything previously seen in children's books. For example, his heavy handed didacticism and scare tactics were countered with brightly colored and therefore engaging pictures, although some of these colorful pictures were every bit as frightening as the text. One is left wondering whether his intent was to scare the child or to humor the child, and there are differing opinions on that matter.

One scholar of children's literature, Eva Maria Metcalf, published her article titled, *Civilizing Manners and Mocking Morality: Dr. Heinrich Hoffmann's Struwwlepeter*, in *The Lion and The Unicorn* in 1996. In this article she states, "*Struwwelpeter* marks the beginning of the modern picture book design through its interplay of picture and text, and it displays a blend of the *popular and pedagogical* [italics added], typical of the modern picture book" (Metcalf, 1996).

The *Struwwelpeter* book was immensely popular and underwent numerous printings, but *pedagogical*, it was not. Its popularity can be attributed to the fact that nothing resembling this had existed on the market prior to 1845, the date of publication. It was therefore novel and for many may have been humorous in its excessive and exaggerated violence. As an example, children growing up in the 1960s may recall the images in Warner Brothers' *Looney Tunes* animation of the proverbial anvil falling on *Wile E. Coyote's* head, flattening him, or a bundle of TNT exploding in his hands, leaving his upper torso scorched and smoking and his head sitting precariously askew on his neck. These are excessively violent acts, but we understood, at the age of six, or eight, or ten, that they were meant to be humorous. It is the exaggeration, or use of hyperbole, that was supposed to transform the violence into something more palatable for children.

But humor, even the perverse kind, is not pedagogy and therefore would land on the *popular* side of the equation, and the *pedagogy* then, must be in the underlying message. However, when the underlying message is didactic in nature it is difficult to consider that message in pedagogical terms. Nevertheless, when we understand the terms *didacticism* and *pedagogy* broadly, we can reason that both terms refer to teaching something. In that instance, pedagogy and didacticism are not mutually exclusive. In fact, didacticism was used deliberately to teach children certain lessons and the use of didacticism in *Struwwelpeter* is quite evident. "In the mid-nineteenth century, educational messages of civility and obedience were the rule in a children's book, and in this regard Hoffmann's *Struwwelpeter* makes no exception" (Metcalf, 1996). Hoffmann's three-year-old son was the impetus for the *Struwwelpeter* stories and Hoffmann's intent in writing the stories was to educate his son.

Didactic or Pedagogically Sound?
Frightening or Entertaining?
Wherein Lies the Difference?

Heinrich Hoffmann is said to have disliked the heavy handed didactic children's books on the market, and thus wrote his own book. The available books, he said, were either stuffy and lifeless or far too sentimental for his tastes. "What he found lacking in these books was the consideration of a child's ability to approach text and illustration and, especially, a child's desire for drama and action" (Metcalf, 1996). Hoffmann set out to write his book with two basic concepts in mind: it should be child centered and it should be highly entertaining. However, Hoffmann was not an early childhood educator nor a writer, but a doctor of psychiatry. He certainly achieved the drama and action he was after, but it is questionable whether these stories were child centered and entertaining, even in nineteenth century Germany.

Consider the story of *Conrad* who gets his thumbs hacked off with steel shears. This is perhaps the epitome of action and drama. Conrad is startled by a grown man who bursts into his home and chases the boy around the living room waving huge sharp scissors. After his thumbs are hacked off Conrad is left weeping, blood spurting from each of his now thumbless hands. Also consider the intended audience for the story: Heinrich Hoffmann's three-year-old son. According to Piaget's developmental theory, a three-year-old child is in the early preoperational stage, egocentric and incapable of thinking beyond their own immediate situation and needs. I would reason that Conrad's story would be terribly frightening to a three-year-old child, but the younger Hoffmann was not the only child to be exposed to the *Struwwelpeter* stories. As the book grew in popularity, older children may have read it independently and may very well have found humor and entertainment in its pages. However, the *Struwwelpeter* stories were originally intended to be read *to* the child, assuming that Hoffmann's three-year-old son could not yet read independently.

The child's ability to approach the text, according to Metcalf, was another of Hoffmann's considerations in writing *Struwwelpeter*. Whether intentional or not, Hoffmann has used strategies for facilitating the young reader's decoding and comprehension skills that are acceptable practices in elementary school classrooms today; in particular, the use of rhyme and pattern. The rhyming patterns aid the young reader by lending an element of predictability to the text. The use of rhyme further assists beginning readers through the use of auditory and visual "chunks," i.e., differing onsets preceding rhymes that look and sound alike:

> See Slovenly Peter! Here he <u>st / ands</u>,
> With his dirty hair and <u>h / ands</u>.

Hoffmann probably did not consider other decoding and comprehension strategies, such as syntax and semantics, or graphophonic analysis (sounding

it out) and "sight words" when writing his stories as he was likely more focused in using the rhyming pattern to enhance the entertainment value of
the story, than he was in using it pedagogically as a decoding and/or comprehension strategy.

"Approaching the text" may also refer to the child's ability to make personal connections to the story, which is the essence of pleasurable reading.
In this sense, Hoffmann has clearly succeeded. In fact, the stories could have
been written as a reaction to behaviors that his child was already exhibiting,
or to those childhood behaviors that Hoffmann anticipated. Every parent
worries for their child's well being and the *Struwwelpeter* stories are, for the
most part, stories of common dangers that befall children—playing with
matches, for example. There is little question that the young reader/listener
can readily relate to the stories, whether the listener is three years old and
just learning about the dangers of fire, or whether the reader is older and has
already played with, thought about playing with, or knows someone who has
played with fire.

The questions then, are whether the stories are an effective teaching tool,
whether children responded to them with fright or delight, and whether they
are developmentally appropriate. These questions are difficult to answer but
comparisons to contemporary children's fare, such as the Saturday morning
cartoon show, invoke some interesting similarities. Whether or not these stories, which are meant to teach a lesson, are effective in their intent depends
largely upon the child's response to the stories. They may be effective because
they are either particularly frightening or particularly humorous, and therefore likely to have stamina, but the didactic tone of the stories belies any pedagogical value.

Theories of Child Development

The study of child development is a relatively young science. Prior to Sigmund Freud (1856–1939) and his ever controversial psychosexual model of
human development, there was Charles Darwin (1809–1882) who believed
that the child was the link between the human and the animal species. Darwin's racial recapitulation model, a combination of evolutionary biology and
embryology, was popularized by his younger contemporaries, Fritz Muller
(1821–1897) and Ernst Haeckel (1834–1919). Did Hoffmann also believe
that children were animal-like in their behavior and so wrote a book that
would tame their animal instincts?

Other noted child development theorists such as G. Stanley Hall
(1844–1924) touted recapitulation as well. Hall believed that the preadoles-

cent child develops best when not forced to follow constraints, but rather to move freely through the continuum of evolution. He believed that the child should be able to experience how one lived in the simian stage, to be able to express his true animal nature prior to the age of six years.

Considering the publication date of *Struwwelpeter* (1844), there was limited research available at that time to draw on regarding the specific study of child development, and on which to judge the story's developmental appropriateness. Freud's model, which was widely known and should certainly have been known to Dr. Hoffmann, consisted of five stages of development in which the child is expected to resolve the conflict between childhood and sexual urges, or else become fixated in one particular stage. Hoffmann's son would have been in Freud's *Anal* stage of development which occurs between the ages of two and three. At this stage the child typically has their first encounter with rules and regulations, and it is the age at which they generally begin toilet training. The child's experience with regulations, and with regulating their bodily functions, is thought to influence their behavior and their reaction to rules and regulations later in life. Being fixated at this stage (being unsuccessful at resolving the conflict) can result in the child being stingy, stubborn, or orderly and/or *messy*. There may be an interesting correlation here; Hoffmann's son was three years old, may have been immersed in toilet training, and the title story is *Slovenly* [messy] *Peter*. Or it may be pure coincidence that his son's age and developmental stage, according to Freud, can be compared to the slovenliness that *Peter* is prone to. We might also make correlations between Freud's *Oral* stage of development and *The Story About the Thumbsucker*, but these correlations, I think, are a stretch in that they are vague connections at best, and only in regard to one or two of the stories. However, Freud's theories may have influenced Hoffmann in a less direct manner, given the assumption that Hoffman would have been aware, on some level, of these theories.

Ulrich Wiedmann, German and English Professor at the Ludwid-Marum-Gymnasium in Pfinztal, Germany, makes some interesting Freudian analyses when he poses the question, "Why is it always girls who burn?" in his article titled, *The Inflammable Maiden: Some Remarks on Naughty Girls*. Cautionary tales abound that feature girls who burn and Hoffmann's Pauline, who plays with matches, burns so completely that all that remains are her little red shoes. The Freudian interpretation is in the erotic connotation associated with words like *flame, burn, spark*, and *ignite*. Wiedmann explains that individuals can be "fired up" for one another, "in heat," or "burning with desire" (Wiedmann, 2000). One's *flame* is one's lover, who can *spark* a romance, and so on. We are all familiar with the phrase, *don't play with fire*, which refers to any dangerous activity, and young girls especially are warned against toying with danger, which often means sexual experimentation or curiosity. Wiedmann infers that Hoffmann's Pauline is erotically heated up. Her little red shoes are a symbol for sexual curiosity.

Following Freud, there came a succession of influential child developmental theorists. Jean Piaget (1896–1980) conceived of four distinct stages of the child's intellectual development, while Margaret Mahler's (1897–1985) six developmental stages attempt to explain how children attain their sense of self. And Erik Erikson (1902–1994) developed a model in eight stages wherein children are confronted with psychological crises which they must resolve.

However, the theories of Charles Darwin and Sigmund Freud appear to be among the most popular and likely the most recognized at the time of the publication of *Struwwelpeter*. Nevertheless I see little, if any, evidence that the theories of either Freud or Darwin were in the forefront of Hoffmann's conscience when he wrote the stories. While we *could* surmise that the stories are somewhat Freudian (*Slovenly* Peter), although not obviously so, and we could further surmise that they are somewhat reminiscent of Darwin's theory, in that children are animal-like, we could also surmise that it is a categorical stretch to use either theory as a lens. Hoffmann, however, was an educated man—a man of science—in fact, a psychiatrist who, by definition, studied the mental, emotional, and behavioral condition of humans. Given this background it seems reasonable to hold Hoffmann accountable for understanding the phrase *developmentally appropriate*, and for using that knowledge in crafting the stories/lessons for his three-year-old son. A three-year-old has not fully separated fantasy from reality which we can easily observe in their belief in goblins, witches, and other mythical beings, and a three-year-old would likely have difficulty understanding the humorous intent of the graphically violent acts depicted in *Struwwelpeter*.

CHAPTER THREE

Violence as Entertainment

The Stories

Some of the *Struwwelpeter* stories seem mild in comparison to others. For example, Slovenly Peter suffers no physical harm, only humiliation. Actually, the reader understands that Peter *should* be ashamed, but it is unclear whether Peter actually feels the shame. Maybe Peter was perfectly happy being dirty, but the message to the reader is that *they* will feel shame if, like Peter, they fail to employ good grooming habits. Peter's story is neither violent nor frightening and may have been purely entertaining, depending on how it is interpreted by the child, and the child's interpretation is heavily influenced by the tone of the adult voice reading the story—lighthearted or disdainful. Together with the adult reader, the child may laugh at Peter's absurd situation, or the child may judge him with derision and scorn. Either way, Peter suffers no physical harm and there is little to be fearful of in his story.

The stories that follow, however, become increasingly harsher. Stories such as *The Story of Little Suck-A-Thumb* and *The Dreadful Story of Pauline and the Matches* are brutally violent in comparison to *Slovenly Peter*. Both Conrad (*Little Suck-A-Thumb*) and Pauline endure extraordinary pain and suffering. Conrad's thumbs are abruptly amputated—and Pauline burns to death, for no other reason than they ignored or disobeyed authority: their mother's advice. Our initial reaction to this level of violence in a child's story is probably shock and disbelief, but we must carefully consider the long legacy of violence in children's entertainment.

One contemporary story containing a comparable level of violence is found in the Warner Brothers' animated cartoon *The Roadrunner*. In one respect, this assessment will seem cognate to comparing apples and oranges, i.e., two incongruent entities: nineteenth century cautionary tales with twentieth century television animation. However, format aside, Hoffmann's *Struwwelpeter* and Warner Brothers' *Looney Tunes* share one striking similarity: violence as entertainment for children.

Perhaps it is the context in which the story is imbedded that determines whether the material is frightening or entertaining and, unlike Warner Brothers' *Wile E. Coyote* cartoon, Hoffmann's Conrad and Pauline are human children in real life settings. Their fates are no less violent than is Wile E. Coyote's, but the coyote's entire context is one of entertaining humor: the Saturday morning cartoon show. Whether that context justifies the violence is a question for another day. This differs from the context of the printed book, however, as a book can be categorized into any number of genres and themes, with the content dictated by the author; some content is violent and some is not. Whatever the context, though, it undoubtedly influences the viewer's and/or reader's reaction.

Other factors that I see contributing to or influencing one's reaction are repetition, style, enculturation, and reason. The *repetition* I refer to is the frequency of the violent act or acts, and by *style* I am referring to the manner in which the characters are presented: cartoon-like or realistic. *Enculturation* is the term I am using to ascertain what is commonplace and usual for the child, and by examining *reason* I mean to clarify the basis for the violence, i.e, what has caused this violence to happen? The following analysis of *context*, *repetition*, *style*, *enculturation*, and *reason* may serve to clarify whether the content of the *Struwwelpeter* stories is frightening or humorous, despite the author's inferred intention, that they are meant to be humorous.

Context in Looney Tunes

Saturday morning cartoon shows have been a staple of many American children since they began airing in the 1960s with shows like *Mighty Mouse*, *Yogi Bear*, and *Top Cat*, with only one, two, or perhaps three broadcast networks to choose from. However, children in the twenty-first century are offered a much greater variety because of cable TV and satellite dishes, and the number of hours that children sit and watch cartoons has increased dramatically over the past forty-plus years. No longer limited to Saturday mornings, children could effectively access their favorite cartoon shows almost twenty-four hours a day, and those children who do watch cartoons understand that they will be entertained and that they will laugh while passively watching the TV set.

Incidentally, most of the literature regarding children and TV watching is focused on physical health and obesity (rather than on the context of humor/violence) and, according to Dr. Kelley Brownell, Obesity Researcher at Yale University, the average American child sees ten thousand advertisements for food per year and an average of one food advertisement every five minutes on Saturday mornings. Most of these ads are for fast food, sugared cereal, soft drinks, and candy, so watching Saturday morning cartoon shows may not be the best choice for children for a variety of reasons.

Context in *Struwwelpeter*

The context of the written story is vastly different from that of children's television, in this case, for two reasons. Firstly, the content of a book can be anything the author imagines, including humor . . . and including violence. It may be serious or lighthearted, frightening or reassuring, didactic or engaging. Therefore, the expectation upon reading a book is very different from the expectation upon viewing a children's cartoon show. We know at the onset to expect humor (albeit sometimes violent humor) from the animated TV cartoon *because* of context. On the contrary, we do *not* necessarily know what to expect from a book until we pick it up to read it, as the reader's response to the content is largely dependent upon the author's style and intent. As an example, one might expect Eve Merriam's picture book titled *Halloween ABC*, or its sequel, *Spooky ABC*, to be a pedagogically sound method of teaching the ABCs by including cute and engaging Halloween-themed illustrations of candy, goblins, and pumpkins. However, the content of these controversial picture books is anything *but* cute with text that describes irresistible red apples that will render the consumer *dead* with one bite.

But even these books, in all their terrifying imagery, are entertaining. What makes them different and why are these books enjoyable, and not the *Struwwelpeter* stories? Again, it is the context that justifies the violent content. Many North American children celebrate Halloween on October 31st by dressing in costume—as witches, goblins, ghosts—and roam their neighborhoods asking for either tricks or treats. It is a night of mischief and a night to be frightened by haunted houses and skeletons. Children who celebrate Halloween anticipate and delight in being frightened on this holiday. *Struwwelpeter* has no such connection to a positive experience. The violence in *Struwwelpeter* is decontextualized and arbitrary.

Secondly, the context of the written story is vastly different from that of contemporary children's television because children's books were a rarer commodity in the nineteenth century than they are today, and therefore they likely had a greater impact on the reader. As well, reading a book is an interactive experience that can elicit a range of reactions depending on the reader's disposition, experience, and background knowledge. As well, the imagination often conjures more vivid imagery than the television screen, the viewing of which is a passive activity.

Repetition in Looney Tunes

Children watching the *Roadrunner* cartoon quickly ascertain that Wile E. Coyote will be crushed by an anvil, blown up by TNT, and/or run over and dismembered by a locomotive repeatedly within a very short span of time, probably no more than one to two minutes into the cartoon show. They will also realize that no sooner is the main character crushed, blown to bits, or dismembered, than he quickly picks himself up and regains his posture, appearing unscathed in the very next frame. No blood has been shed and he appears impervious to the pain—following a fleeting moment where he may be shown reeling from dizziness or perhaps smoldering. This rapid succession of brutality and recovery, brutality and recovery, may serve to desensitize the viewer who is led to understand that these violent acts cannot be real, and are merely designed for the supposed "entertainment" of the viewer.

Repetition in *Struwwelpeter*

Children reading (or being read to) the *Struwwelpeter* stories are not exposed to that same pattern of brutality and recovery. The acts of violence bestowed upon Hoffmann's characters are one-time occurrences with permanent effects. There is no recovery in sight for these poor children. Conrad's thumbs do not grow back (*Snip! Snap! Snip! They go so fast, that both his thumbs are off at last.*), and Pauline's ashes do not regenerate into human flesh (*So she was burnt with all her clothes, and arms and hands, and eyes and nose.*). The dramatic repercussions of the character's one-time disobedience are swift and irreversible. They do not magically revert back to their former selves. The final illustrations in their stories depict Conrad crying and bleeding, and Pauline's pet cats weeping over her ashes. The finality of their respective fates is irrefutable and frighteningly real.

Style in Looney Tunes

Wile E. Coyote is presented as a highly stylized cartoon. That is, he is rendered by the animator to resemble a coyote, but when compared to an actual coyote, is closer to a caricature of the real thing, than he is to a real coyote. He is portrayed with exaggerated features: huge bulging eyes, floppy oversized ears, and an elongated and crooked snout. His overstated paws, which function more like hands and feet, are attached to an emaciated skeleton-like frame. His diminutive frame is dissimilar to his outsized extremities. Furthermore, his behavior is unlike that of a real coyote; he walks upright, reads complicated diagrams, and concocts complex contraptions in his failed attempts to capture his nemesis, the Roadrunner. His actions and reactions are also exaggerated and are unlike the actions and reactions of real people/real coyotes. He is subjected to the most odious and violent acts, yet emerges reasonably intact. For example, following a direct encounter with an exploding bundle of TNT, he might be seen seething, staggering, or shaking, perhaps with a flock of birds or a ring of stars circling his head, but he is alive and will recover before the next commercial interruption. No human would survive a similar episode.

Style in Struwwelpeter

Peter, Conrad, Pauline, and the other characters portrayed by Hoffmann are rendered in animation as well, but not as caricatures. They are representational depictions of real life children in real life settings. They are proportionately accurate, behave in a realistically human manner, and are set against real life backdrops. They look, speak, and act like real people. Unlike cartoon caricatures, these literary characters lend a frightening realism to the story that is absent in the Saturday morning cartoon show. Peter, Conrad, and Pauline could all live next door to the reader.

Reason in Looney Tunes

Wile E. Coyote and the Roadrunner share a long legacy of violence. They are arch rivals whose never ending conflict persists from one episode to the next. Children viewing the cartoon understand this. Their skirmishes are the very basis for the cartoon and fundamental to its storyline. The Roadrunner is Wile E. Coyote's nemesis and the coyote devotes his every waking hour to capturing him. He fails at each attempt however, for once the Roadrunner is captured the story will end. The reason for the violence lies at the very heart of this story. The violence *is* the story. They are at war. They are natural enemies.

Reason in Struwwelpeter

Conrad, Pauline, and the others fall victim to violence for a more immediate reason; it is because they have ignored their mother's advice. There is no history leading up to, or justifying the violence (if violence can be justified). They have simply disobeyed, which children often do. More specifically, they have not practiced blind obedience to arbitrary authority. Disobedience in children can be viewed as unacceptable or objectionable behavior, or it can be viewed as a learning mode. As adults, many of us expect that children will disobey, for this is one way for them to understand and to learn something new, to experience it first hand. The parents of Conrad and Pauline apparently do not share the same expectation. These parents offer one warning to their children:

> Conrad: *"But mind now Conrad what I say, don't suck your thumb while I'm away."*
> Pauline: *"You'll burn to death, if you do so. Your parents have forbidden you, you know. But Pauline would not take advice, She lit a match, it was so nice!"*

The warning is ignored and the children suffer immediate and unspeakable pain, the effects of which are irreversible. On some level, children who understand that coyotes crushed by anvils cannot really assume the shape of an accordion before regenerating (fantasy), also understand that amputated thumbs and burned flesh simply do *not* regenerate (reality). The reader further understands that they too will suffer similar repercussions for disobedience to a parent.

Enculturation in Looney Tunes

Most American children grow up in a home where one or more television sets are present. According to the U.S. Census Bureau, the number of television sets in U.S. households in 2001 was 248 million, the percentage of households with at least one TV in 2001 was 98.2 percent and the average number of TVs per home in 2001 was 2.4. Hence, most American children are familiar with popular TV shows and their formats. Children learn that the Saturday morning cartoon show, for example, is dramatically different from a documentary or news cast.

Enculturation in Struwwelpeter

Books, especially children's books, were a rarer commodity in the nineteenth century home than they are today, and picture books, such as *Struwwelpeter*, however popular, were a novelty; not every household contained children's books. If the printed word is powerful, then I imagine it was all the more powerful when books were such valuable commodities. Whether entertaining or frightening, the *Struwwelpeter* stories undoubtedly had a tremendous impact on children.

The child's response to a written story—or a viewed cartoon—is dependent upon many variables and no two children will perceive the text or the cartoon in exactly the same manner. However, based on the criteria of context, repetition, style, enculturation, and reason, it seems that the *Struwwelpeter* stories would be perceived as frightening to many children as there is little indication that humor is present or intended in the stories.

Humor

Humor is defined as that which is intended to induce laughter or amusement. While the word *laugh* or *laughter* is present in four of the *Struwwelpeter* stories, this laughter is targeted *at* the victim, which the astute reader interprets more as cruelty than as humor. To laugh *with* someone is humorous, to laugh *at* someone is not, particularly when the recipient of the laughter is ill, has had a mishap, or identifies with a marginalized population, which is the case in three of the four *Struwwelpeter* stories in which laughter is present.

1. Illness: In *The Story of Cruel Frederick*, Frederick's dog Tray *laughs* when he sees the pies and puddings left by Frederick, which Tray can now eat himself, because Frederick is bedridden after being bitten by Tray. The laughter is not light-heartedly humorous, but mean spirited and vindictive. Both Frederick and his dog Tray have caused each other harm, and Tray is laughing because his revenge is sweet which, ironically, seems no laughing matter.

2. Marginalized populations: In *The Story of the Inky Boys*, the "naughty" [white] boys *laugh* at the "Black-a-moor" while singing, "Oh Blacky, you're as black as ink." The White boys laugh at the Black child for no other reason than his skin is black. The situation is a complex one; the reader is being warned against teasing the "Black-a-moor" (sic) because such racially biased behavior is inappropriate, but no mention is made of the pejorative racial slurs imbedded in the text, which apparently *are* appropriate in the eyes of the author. Here the laughter is targeted at a marginalized population who is further subjugated by the context of the story.

3. Mishap: In *The Story of Johnny Look-In-The-Air*, Johnny falls into the river and loses his writing book. Two men pull him out with a hook and describe him as being in a *sorry plight, dripping wet, and such a fright.* Just as he's being pulled from the river the fish come up *to enjoy the fun and laughter.* They are *laughing at* Johnny because of the miserable condition he is in, which is malicious.

4. The final story in which laughter appears is *The Story of the Wild Huntsman*. In many ways this story differs from the others. There is no *naughty* child who misbehaves and is then punished. Instead, a nearsighted

hunter in a green jacket attempts to *shoot the hares and kill them dead.* But the crafty hare outwits him. *The hare sits snug in leaves and grass and laughs to see the green man pass.* The hare steals the hunter's gun when the hunter falls asleep and, upon waking, the hunter is looking down the barrel of his own weapon. The hunter is frightened, stumbles backwards, and falls into the well. The hare pulls the trigger, misses the hunter, and instead hits the coffee cup that the hunter's wife is holding, spilling hot coffee all over her. This story unfolds in a chain of mishaps that *are* humorous, and we can laugh at the role reversal of the hunter and the hare. Justice is served with no children being killed, maimed, or humiliated.

A Manual of Good Sense?

A recent publication titled *Struwwelpeter: Fearful Stories & Vile Pictures to Instruct Good Little Folks,* is written as a parody of the original publication by Heinrich Hoffmann, and extols the entertainment value of the stories. In the introduction written by Jack Zipes, a respected scholar of children's literature, it is stated, "The soothing playful voice that speaks in rhymes in all of Hoffmann's books seeks to convince and seduce the child reader into heeding the advice illustrated by the pictures" (Zipes, 1999, p. 8). This soothing voice, as interpreted by Zipes, is the same voice that places Conrad's mother in collusion with the enemy in *Little Suck-A-Thumb* and looks upon the characters in the remaining stories with condescension and disdain.

Perhaps the *soothing voice* that Zipes refers to is to be found in the *format* of the stories—the rhyming couplets—for I find very little in the content of the stories that is soothing. The content, when compared to the rhyming scheme which has a pleasing sing-song appeal to it, is dramatically contradictory. The stories are a confusion of menacing warnings couched in child-friendly rhymes.

Zipes calls *Struwwelpeter* a "funny manual of good sense." He says, "It is not nonsensical, as some critics have claimed. Rather, it is eminently reasonable and straightforward. Without pretension it tells children, especially middle class children, exactly what will happen to them in graphic detail if they do not do as they are told" (Zipes, 1999, p. 8). *Eminently reasonable* is not a phrase that I would use to describe the violent passages from *Struwwelpeter* that describe cruelty to animals and dismemberment and death of children:

With fright she shrieks and tries to run, but ah! 'tis all in vain . . .
Then you should have been by to see how Fred did scream and cry . . .

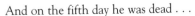

And on the fifth day he was dead . . .
But oh! To hear her scream and cry their inmost souls did harrow . . .
They stung, they bit him foot and head, nor left him till he fell quite dead . . .
When they looked at her head, they thought she was dead . . .
Fritz never saw the light again . . .
Then at our Hugo's leg he flew, and made him shriek with pain . . .
They never saw their child again . . .
The pigs and the dogs ate him up in the gutter . . .
His body on the floor was hurled, and all that was left was a lock of his hair . . .

These passages are but a few from the (eventual) thirty-eight *Struwwelpeter* stories, and without a doubt tell children exactly what will happen to them if they disobey. Zipes considers the straightforward manner in which these punishments are described to be unpretentious, but I don't think that *unpretentious* adequately describes the extreme candor in the message. Is it necessary to amputate the character's thumbs in order to encourage the reader to discontinue their thumb sucking? Why thumbsucking is considered naughty is also debatable, but the topic in question is the method, not the act. To refer to these stories as a "funny manual" remains an area of uncertainty for me, yet Zipes is not the only scholar to see the humor in *Struwwelpeter*.

According to Adam Parfrey, editor at Feral House Publishing, publisher of the parody, *Struwwelpeter, Fearful Stories and Vile Pictures to Instruct Good Little Folks* (1999), "Mr. Zipes finally does away with a long held reactionary opinion about the harmful aspects of *Struwwelpeter*. Zipes now believes that, even if gruesome, *Struwwelpeter* was originally intended to create an entertaining lesson for children by a loving father" (Parfrey, 1999).

And gruesome they are. The *Struwwelpeter* parody published by Feral House capitalizes on the grisly and macabre qualities that have made *Struwwelpeter* famous. While the text remains true to the original, the illustrations by Sarita Vendetta are ghastly. Slovenly Peter is depicted as a disfigured ogre. His finger and toe nails are thick and gnarled, his eyes sunken and rheumy, his face ulcerated. His posture is animal-like and his clothing is torn, dirty, and barely held together with pins, sticks, and some crude stitching. Yet Peter, slovenly as he appears, is among the least offensive and frightening of the illustrations in this parody.

The second story, *The Dreadful Story of Pauline and the Matches*, portrays Pauline in a triptych-like format—three images of Pauline that form the eyes and nose of a human skull, with her cat howling ferociously at the top. The first image of Pauline (the left eye of the skull) shows her in a resolute state, about to strike the match. She leans into the act, her brow furrowed and her lip curled. She is determined to create fire. The second image (the right eye of the skull) depicts a girl engulfed in flames. Her hollow eyes seem to scream as her mouth gapes open and her arms reach out for help. The final image (the mouth of the skull) is a charred image of blackened flesh, no hair, and hollow sunken eye sockets.

The illustrations are disturbing at best, and by the publisher's own admission, not meant for the eyes of children. The book's characters are shown screaming and bleeding. Babies are being pecked to death by birds and tortured by insects. Bodies are dismembered and disfigured. Small animals are forced through meat grinders and adults are shown in aberrant sexual situations. But after all, this is merely a parody, and not the real thing. The disturbing effect of the *real thing* is much more subtle.

Comparisons

Although the Feral House parody of *Struwwelpeter* is clearly not meant for children, many good children's books contain violent content and place their characters in miserable situations, and there is a certain interest, even a fascination with this subject matter among some readers. Consider Roald Dahl's characters who espouse the values of genius, courage, and practicality while opposing overindulgences such as sloth and greed. Some say the characters from Dahl's *Charlie and the Chocolate Factory* were inspired by the characters in Hoffmann's *Struwwelpeter*. Dahl's stories feature some of the most neglected, abused, tormented, and long-suffering characters that we encounter in the literary canon. Dahl's own childhood experience was harrowing and traumatic, and he may have drawn on real life experience—or perceived experience—to develop his literary characters, but could have also been influenced by or drawn to the suffering endured by Hoffmann's characters. "What makes Dahl's works for young audiences so appealing is the clever, macabre, wish fulfillment in his adult fare scaled to the gratification of children" (Galef, D., 1996).

Some individuals have compared the fates of the secondary characters in Dahl's *Charlie and the Chocolate Factory* with the fates of the characters in Hoffmann's *Struwwelpeter* declaring an unmistakable resemblance between the two. However, this *unmistakable* resemblance is only evident in the ultimate fate and/or demise of the characters, and not necessarily in the characters themselves. For example, the Dahl characters that have been compared to Hoffmann's characters are all secondary characters—antagonists that we meet once we're inside the chocolate factory—while Hoffmann's characters are all protagonists—main characters. Often times the Hoffmann characters are the *only* character in the story, and not well developed—which may be a commonality with Dahl's secondary characters. But of course there is a valid literary reason why Dahl's secondary characters are not well developed—because they are *secondary* characters. Inside Dahl's chocolate factory we meet Augustus Gloop, an overweight boy who values food above all else; Veruca Salt, a demanding child who throws tantrums until her parents give her what she wants; Violet Beauregarde, a wise-cracking character and avid gum chewer; and Mike Teevee, a rambunctious boy who cares only for television.

Like Hoffmann's characters, Dahl's child characters are all punished in violent ways for their misguided behaviors, but the reader does not relate to them the way they relate to the main character, Charlie, who is well developed. The secondary characters are meant only to stand in contrast to the main character. Furthermore, Hoffmann's characters are not all loathsome and obnoxious children, as are the children we meet inside Dahl's chocolate factory. Although *some* are . . . such as Cruel Frederick who we are *told* is cruel in the title of his story. Others are just mischievous, absentminded, fidgety, or unkempt, unlike Dahl's characters, who maintain dubious values, such as Veruca Salt who audaciously places unreasonable demands on her parents by adamantly insisting she get her way.

There is, however, one interesting correlation among both sets of characters. Augustus Gloop and *Augustus Who Would Not Have Any Soup* exemplify the correlation. Hoffmann's Augustus *refused* to eat and Dahl's Augustus would not *stop* eating. Their problems are antithetical. As well they share the same first name and have a rhyming component to their names: *Gloop* and *Soup*.

While Hoffmann placed no emphasis on developing his literary characters, Dahl creates main characters that are believable and with whom the reader can make a personal connection. From the impoverished Charlie in *Charlie and the Chocolate Factory*, to the neglected James in *James and the Giant Peach*, we encounter literary characters who face some of life's most challenging obstacles with valor and resolve. Dahl's main characters are often orphaned, sometimes as the result of their parents being brutally murdered, and are sent to live with cruel or incapable relatives who are unable or unwilling to meet the needs of these children. They are neglected, starved, and abused, and they are really quite different from the characters in *Struwwelpeter*. Dahl's well developed characters are set in a literary context where they struggle with universal conflicts over good and evil, and eventually overcome enormous obstacles to emerge as emotionally whole beings. The plots and the characters' actions in Dahl's books ring true with an internal logic that appeals to the intelligent reader's emotions and mirrors the human experience.

A more current example of suffering protagonists appears in the *Lemony Snicket's A Series of Unfortunate Events* books which have recently become popularized through Paramount Picture's movie production. These dark stories feature the three Baudelaire children who are playing on the beach when a Mr. Poe approaches to deliver the message that their parents have perished in a fire. The children are subsequently sent to live a dreadful existence with the dastardly Count Olaf where they endure abhorrent living conditions.

And then there is the Harry Potter series written by J. K. Rowling. The inimitable Harry Potter suffers intolerable abuses at the hand of his ignorant relatives, the Dursleys, following the untimely death of his birth parents. Harry's poor treatment at the hands of his aunt and uncle Dursley is amplified by the pampering that they bestow upon their own son: Harry's cousin Dudley. The contrast in treatment of the two boys serves to magnify the abuse that Harry suffers.

In some respect, these literary characters suffer all the abuses and neglect of the *Struwwelpeter* characters, but the differences are evident. Charlie Bucket, Harry Potter, and the Baudelaire orphans suffer abuse and neglect from truly evil villains and these outside forces are eventually punished for their misdeeds. Justice prevails. Punishing the evil forces offers the young reader a satisfying closure that is congruent with Lawrence Kohlberg's theory of moral development in children. Children in the preconventional stage of their moral development believe that evil behavior will be punished and that good behavior is the result of obedience, or of avoidance of the evil implicit in disobedience (Power et al., 1989).

Hoffmann's characters are punished for disobedience to authority rather than as victims of their circumstances, a notion that is similarly congruent with Kohlberg's theory, but quite a different circumstance for the literary character. The characters, the punishments, and the situations are all vastly dissimilar:

Characters

The characters in these contemporary stories by Dahl, Rowling, and Snicket are well developed, believable, and realistic characters that the reader can relate to on a personal and meaningful level. Their experiences touch the human spirit. We care about them, we root for them, and we live vicariously through them as we turn each page.

Conversely, the characters in Hoffman's book are flat, one dimensional, "cardboard cut-outs" of children. They have no dimension or depth beyond the single facet of their personality—disobedience—around which the entire story flows. They appear for one reason only, to warn the reader against similar disobedience.

Punishments

Contemporary characters such as Charlie Bucket, the Baudelaire orphans, and Harry Potter suffer punishment and abuse, but not necessarily related to their actions. Their punishment is largely unfounded, something that has been unfairly bestowed upon them by evil characters. They have our deepest sympathy and support as they demonstrate the strength of character that allows them to overcome their oppression. There is a fulfilling sense of healing in the story's resolution.

The *Struwwelpeter* characters suffer punishment as well, but their punishment is swift and irreversible, a direct product of their disobedience to authority. There is no recovery for Hoffmann's victims, nor are they allowed any flexibility—no second chances, no forgiveness, no deals struck. They disobey and suffer the consequence.

Situation

Dahl, Rowling, and Snicket create rich settings and intriguing plots in which their well developed characters operate. This affords the reader a contextual framework in which to make judgments and formulate opinions about the characters and their actions. As well, these stories have an internal logic that validates the character's actions, lends credence to their situation, and encourages the reader to make a personal connection with the characters and their plights. These books have literary value and can stand alone on their literary merit.

The legacy of violence in children's literature is as apparent as the disparity in the violence between traditional and contemporary literature for children. The violent content in the traditional stories, such as the cautionary tales written by Hoffmann or the brothers Grimm, is overtly didactic and somewhat gratuitous, and meant to frighten children into behaving properly. This is unlike the violence in contemporary children's literature which is imbedded within a rich literary context that allows the reader to engage in critical thinking and to imagine lives and circumstances beyond their own existence.

The situations warranting punishment in *Struwwelpeter* are arbitrary. There is little, if any, character development, plot, or setting. The story is no more than a blatant warning to children. The violence bestowed upon the

Struwwelpeter characters is merely a sadistic warning to the reader against misbehavior, unlike the violence suffered by the Dahl, Snicket, and Rowling characters. These authors create contemporary characters that are models for resisting oppression and abuse and find within themselves the strength and courage to cope with their desperate situations. Contemporary children's literature that is well written offers the reader a satisfactory closure, even if the conflict remains open-ended, and reassures the reader that they too can overcome life's obstacles.

CHAPTER FOUR

The *Struwwelpeter* Stories

The Cautionary Tale Motif

Cautionary tales can be distinguished by the author's heavy-handed and overt didacticism, often spelling out to the reader both the moral of the story and the consequence of misbehavior. With little or no focus on literary quality—plot, characterization, setting, theme, style, or point of view—the characters are flat and one dimensional and the events linear. These stories generally follow a simple pattern of *misdeed and punishment*, a favorite theme of nineteenth century authors of children's stories. The purpose of the cautionary tale is not to entertain its readers, but to frighten them into proper behavior by graphically relating the sadistic and gruesome consequences of misbehavior. "It seems there must always be something Germanic about perversity, gloom, and torture in the arts" (Zipes, 2001).

Although Zipes's commentary is in reference to the junk opera titled *Shockheaded Peter* performed by The Tiger Lillies, which was inspired by "some gruesome tales from the most famous German children's book in the world: *Der Struwwelpeter*" (Zipes, 2001), perversity, gloom, and torture are also evident in the Germanic folk and fairy tales which often use gruesome scare tactics to frighten and/or control children, the same tactics that have been used for centuries. The Ancient Greeks had the black birds *Lamia* and *Striga* who, like their Hebrew counterpart, *Lilith*, ate children raw and drank their blood. According to deMause, these characters and others like them were invented for the child's benefit to make them "less rash and ungovernable" (deMause).

Most ancients agreed that it was good to have the images of witches constantly before children, to let them feel the terror of waiting up at night for ghosts to steal them away, eat them, tear them to pieces, and suck their blood or their bone marrow (deMause, 1974, p. 11).

DeMause is quoting to the words of Dio Chrysostom, a Greek philosopher and historian of the first Roman Empire who lived from 40 AD to 120 AD; eighty of his *Discourses* remain in existence today.

By medieval times witches and devils took center stage in children's stories with an occasional Jew thrown in as a cutter of babies' throats. And after the Reformation, God himself prevailed as the primary source of fodder used for terrifying children. One written account describing the tortures God had in store for children in Hell depicts a God who holds the child over the pit of hell and reads, "The little child is in this red-hot oven. Hear how it screams to come out . . . It stamps its little feet on the floor" (deMause, 1974, p. 12).

Traditional scare tactics, however, have given way to more humane child rearing practices. As an example: upon observing a modern American childcare center in a large metropolitan area, affiliated with a major research university, and which enjoys an outstanding national reputation and abides by an explicit progressive philosophy (Savelsberg, 1996), Joachim Savelsberg, Professor of Sociology at the University of Minnesota, makes some patent comparisons between discipline practices evidenced in the *Struwwelpeter* stories and discipline practices in the modern childcare center. The similarities and differences in these discipline practices are evident; while societal norms for proper behavior have changed little, the sanctions have changed dramatically. At the core of the childcare center's philosophy are the guiding principles of: cultural and racial pluralism, nonviolence, and physical safety, among others. Similarly, the *Struwwelpeter* stories address racial tolerance, nonviolence, and physical safety, but do so in a rather duplicitous manner.

While the rules at the childcare center have a direct correlation to the societal norms and rules addressed in *Struwwelpeter*, it is in the execution of the sanctions where the considerable differences lie—a major difference being that *Struwwelpeter* addresses childhood behavior and/or misbehavior in a prohibitive manner while the childcare center addresses the same issues using a more supportive model.

Savelsberg's sociological approach to his analysis of the *Struwwelpeter* collection of stories is focused primarily on society's responses to bad deeds. The traditional sanctions imposed on the evildoers in *Struwwelpeter* appear barbaric when compared to the more progressive techniques practiced by many parents and educators today, techniques that could be categorized as post-modern because of their distinct focus on issues of social justice.

While some of the scholars who have analyzed the *Struwwelpeter* stories actually fear that *Struwwelpeter* has become a "cultural icon of its original meaning, message, and connotations, ready to become a part of the post-modern play of allusions" (Metcalf, 1996), a comparison between traditional and postmodern child rearing practices affords a greater insight into Hoffmann's impetus and objectives for writing these stories and begins to address some of the questions posed in Chapter I. But Metcalf's statement, I believe, is based on the existence of a preponderance of parodies, parodies of parodies, spin-offs, and imitations based on the original *Struwwelpeter*, and not on the analysis of the text or illustrations.

Savelsberg uses three of the childcare center's primary philosophical components to compare modern and traditional discipline practices; i.e., a comparison of childcare center practices with societal norms evidenced in *Struwwelpeter*. In *Struwwelpeter*, the Inky Boys ridicule Black people for having black skin. The White boys are then dipped in black ink with the understanding that they too will experience the feeling of being ridiculed for the color of their skin. The sanction itself is inherently racist. The reader understands that once the boys have been dipped into ink and transformed into Black people, they too will be ridiculed. The underlying message is that Black people will, or should, or might be ridiculed simply because they're Black, but that we should not engage in such behavior because it is rude. The sanction addresses the societal norm of politeness, but wholly ignores any recognition of racism. The reader could assume that racism is acceptable so long as it is not publicly demonstrated, or that rude behavior is the more serious offense as compared to racism.

This is vastly different, philosophically, from a typical sanction at the childcare center where a child who ridicules another for being different is reminded not to use "hurtful words" and would be "encouraged to grasp the value of the coexistence of difference" (Savelsberg, 1996). The childcare center uses words to address the sanction, words that have an educational component. Sanctions in *Struwwelpeter* use physical actions, often violent ones, and the offender, in this case, is treated in the same offensive manner as was their victim, with an *eye for an eye* mentality.

Gentle touches is indicative of another of the childcare center's core values and pertains to its nonviolent philosophical component. In *Struwwelpeter* we find physically violent responses to children's misbehavior, unlike a typical response in the childcare center where words are used to respond to deviance from the rules, or in more extreme cases, a separation or time-out.

Finally, physical safety is at the core of both the childcare center's philosophy and the *Struwwelpter* stories' message. In *Struwwelpeter* children are warned against playing with matches and reminded to watch where they're going. Children who ignore or disobey these directives are met with violent penalties, while children at the childcare center who ignore or disobey these same rules are reminded with words to follow the rules. For example, children in the childcare center are reminded to use "walking feet," unlike Robert in *The Story of Flying Robert* who disobeys and was never seen again.

Furthermore, the childcare center that Savelsberg uses in his comparison gives children choices. These children decide for themselves how much food to consume at mealtime. They are not pressured into finishing their meals, nor are they expected to sit perfectly still through an entire meal, unlike Augustus or Fidgety Philip whose parents demand, unsuccessfully, that they sit still and clean their dinner plates.

Modern society has moved away from using physical force as their primary problem solving mode, as was the common practice in medieval times. Such means have become institutionalized and the use of force by individuals is no longer considered to be acceptable civilized behavior; self control is the current societal expectation. Books of etiquette appeared as early as the thirteenth century with edicts such as this one: "When you blow your nose or cough, turn around so that nothing falls on the table" (Elias, 1979). While these rules of social conduct were intended for persons of royal blood, by the nineteenth century they had eventually filtered down to apply as an expectation to all people.

As newly accepted practices of deportment emerged and spread throughout society, so were these norms reflected in the literature. In the years preceding the publication of *Struwwelpeter*, Frankfurt, Germany, underwent a dramatic transformation with the emergence of a new bourgeois society. In addition to political, economic, and social change, Frankfurt's educational system experienced sweeping reforms with the development of their new public school model, the *Volksschulen* wherein each class served one hundred children and classroom management was likely an overwhelming undertaking. When we consider the publication of *Struwwelpeter* against this rapidly changing landscape, one can begin to understand the need for control of their children.

Hitler's Youth

As a child Nancy Sommers, an English Professor of college composition, remembers hearing the *horrid Struwwelpeter* stories from her parents, stories with crystal clear moral lessons whose exhortations urged her to abide by her parents' wishes. "Do the right thing, they said; obey authority, or else cata-strophic things—dissipation, suffocation, loss of thumbs—will follow" (Sommers, 1992). It never occurred to Sommers to wonder why her parents, who had escaped Nazi Germany in 1939, "were so deferential to authority, so beholden to sanctioned sources of power" (Sommers, 1992). Nor, as Sommers observes, did it occur to her parents to make the connection between generations of German children reading *Struwwelpeter*, who are instructed from early childhood to defer to parental authority, and the Nazis' seemingly effortless rise to power.

Hitler recognized the power of influencing young German boys and girls to insure the continued vitality of his Thousand Year Reich and indoctrinated a generation of German children with racist Nazi ideology. The tactics used on Hitler's Youth was based on the inculcation of values through repetition, brainwashing, and chanting. Children whose personalities were newly developing were easy prey and naturally drawn to the strong sense of belonging and structure, much like the Boy Scouts and Girl Scouts of America, that being a member of Hitler's Youth offered. Even those children who were excluded under Nazi ideology, such as Jewish children, envied the rituals—flag raisings, marching in step, and Nazi Party holidays complete with huge bonfires and bombastic speeches, which were set in opposition to religious holidays. All of it was a recipe for seduction and for eradication of independent thought. Children were sworn in, promising to devote their lives to Hitler—adolescent girls even sent love letters to him.

Perhaps we can understand this irrational passion when we compare it to the Beatle-mania that swept the United States in the 1960s. Girls fainted at the sight of the Beatles, sent love letters to the band members, and dreamed of marrying their favorite Beatle. Young people have a strong desire to be a part of something larger and to be like others: to fit in and to conform. This concept was at the core of Hitler's Youth organizations. Aryan male children became a part of the *Deutches Jungvolk*, or *German Young People*, and females became a part of the *Bund Deutscher Madel*, or *League of German Girls*. Males were trained for dedication, fellowship, and Nazi conformity while girls were trained for comradeship, domestic duties, and motherhood.

Deference to authority—parental, institutional, or political—has long been a societal expectation and Germany's *Struwwelpeter* maintains that legacy in its ideological assumption of deference to arbitrary authority.

Illustrative Technique

While the original illustrations were rendered in a more exaggerated style than all subsequent editions, they were nevertheless realistically rendered.

Many argue that it was the caricaturistic nature of the illustrations that assured the young reader that the stories were humorous, as it was obviously not the terrifying text. However, the illustrations in subsequent editions have not changed dramatically from the originals. The tailor, for example, in *The Story of Little Suck-A-Thumb*, appears in the original text with impossibly thin legs. This image remained unchanged from the original publication date of 1854 until the second edition, published in 1858 when the tailor became plumper and hence, more realistic, although still quite thin.

Hoffmann's second version is distinguished by much more realism and artistic refinement . . . whereas previous illustrations were simple and admittedly "dilettantish" (Sauer, 2003). The new illustrations were more carefully composed and included richer details along with background scenery.

The original image of the exaggeratedly thin tailor may have appeared humorous to his audience of nineteenth century German children who previously had only been exposed to rigidly representational depictions of everyday objects in their illustrated children's books, which of course, was Hoffmann's purported impetus for writing and illustrating his own children's book. However, the humor in the exaggerated illustrations hardly overshadows the disturbing violence in the content of the story, and each subsequent printing of the text depicted more realistically rendered characters. In fact, some say that professional artists were enlisted to illustrate portions of later editions, under Hoffmann's supervision.

Eva Marie Metcalf describes Hoffmann's illustrations as *cartoon-like* and states that "the nature of the drawings helps readers keep fiction and reality apart" (Metcalf, 1996). She admits, however, that "some three-year-olds may still be scared rather than amused by the tailor storming in with his huge scissors ready to cut off Konrad's thumbs" (Metcalf, 1996). Metcalf, I think, is correct in her assumption; the image is terrifying. In any case, the pictures, she says, are *dynamic* and provide *thrill and excitement for the young audience* (Metcalf, 1996). Perhaps Metcalf is suggesting that the illustrations are *thrilling* and *exciting* in the way a roller coaster ride is thrilling and exciting; the passenger rides slowly up a long incline until they are suddenly thrust over the summit into a sheer vertical plunge. The thrill and excitement originate from a combination of panic, amusement, and fear. Yet Hoffmann's illustrations are not a roller coaster ride, but two dimensional representations of actions. The reader observes the illustration rather than physically experiencing it, and the very young child is even further removed from it as they are being read *to*, and may see the illustration only *after* the passage has been read. While the cartoon-like quality of the illustrations serve to diminish the terrifying nature of the text, it is unlikely that very young audiences would make clear distinctions between cartoon-*like* renderings and representational illustrations.

Hoffmann's illustrations have been praised for their appeal as the forerunner of comics and cartoons for children, and have been credited for *Struwwelpeter*'s lasting appeal. Maurice Sendak, one of America's premier author/illustrators of children's literature has called *Struwwelpeter* one of the most beautiful books in the world. Sendak's commendation is in reference to the expressive quality of the simple drawings that draw the attention of the young reader, which were quite unlike anything previously known at that time.

University Professor Walter Sauer notes that, because Hoffmann wrote *Struwwelpeter* for his three-year-old son, the stories became biographical, or are "based on biographical sources provided by the author [himself]" (Sauer, 2003). This, he says, is a significant distinction between *Struwwelpeter* and other works of fiction by Hoffmann's contemporaries. However, Hoffmann admits to producing the cartoon drawings that appear in *Struwwelpeter*, for his young patients—to calm their fears—and Sauer observes that "Hoffmann himself admits that some of the stories, especially the main hero, grew on practical soil" (Sauer, 2003). We can interpret this to mean that the stories, or at least the illustrations, were borne of practical necessity—that of calming his young patients—and not conceived of as a gift for Hoffmann's young son Carl at all.

Sauer recognizes the prevailing story of *Struwwelpeter*'s origins as mythology, with the actual story being far less romantic. The conventional story is that Hoffmann wished to purchase a book for his son, was frustrated by the apparent didacticism in the available selection of books, and so purchased a blank note book and rushed home to his astonished wife to declare his intention to write his own picture book, and to have it completed in time to place under the Christmas tree.

The reality, however, may be less dramatic. It is entirely possible that the book evolved much more slowly, over long periods of time and Hoffmann has contradicted himself on the subject of the inception of the book. In written testimonies, such as those associated with court cases involving imitations and publication rights, Hoffmann stated that the pictures were drawn for his young patients and that they preceded the text. At other times, such as in the Foreword of published editions of *Struwwelpeter*, Hoffmann recites the more romantic version of the story, describing how his frustration with existing books led him to rush home to write his own story just in time for Christmas. It is difficult to determine the truth; in many of the illustrations the text fits neatly into text boxes which are imbedded in the illustrations, and therefore could not have preceded the text.

Whether or not the prevailing notions of the origins of the story are mythical or factual may remain a mystery, but existing early editions of the manuscript leave no question that contextual changes were made prior to publication. Hoffmann's original drawing of Cruel Frederick, for example, depicts a "heavy flow of red blood gushing out of Frederick's uplifted leg and later trickling out from under his bedclothes and onto the floor" (Sauer, 2003). As well, Conrad shed copious amounts of blood following his thumb amputation. Both illustrations were altered prior to publication. Speculation as to why Hoffmann second guessed the liberal use of blood and gore are threefold; Hoffmann may have realized that the abundance of blood was excessive for an audience of young readers, Hoffmann's publisher may have objected to the bloody scenes, and Hoffmann's young son may have been upset by the blood-drenched illustrations.

And there were other changes as well. Conrad's name was changed from the original *Peter*, the *Black-A-Moor's* color was changed from gray to black, illustrations of Christmas trees appeared in the *Foreword* section, and so on. In fact, Walter Sauer offers a meticulously detailed account of the alterations made in each subsequent edition of *Struwwelpeter* from changes in text and illustrations, to changes in format, number of pages, and binding and printing techniques.

One particularly interesting change occurred prior to the first published edition, in *The Story of Cruel Frederick*. Frederick's dog is said to be eating *den guten Gunging* (the good cake). However, *Gunging* was changed to *Kuchen* prior to printing as there is no word in the German language that is spelled g-u-n-g-i-n-g. *Gunging* may have been a mispronunciation of *Kuchen*, the manner in which Hoffmann's son pronounced *kuchen* in his baby talk, and Hoffmann may have used the term in his book as an inside family joke (Sauer, 2003).

Struwwelpeter

The *Struwwelpeter* stories contained in this chapter are the English translation of the original German text; the ten stories appeared in the early issues of *Struwwelpeter*. The original stories were all titled similarly; each title began with *The Story About . . .* , and then gave a child's name or a theme. However, the format of the book became rather awkward with each subsequent publication and appears to be somewhat randomly designed rather than deliberately put into *parallel construction*.

The principle of parallel construction requires that expressions of similar content and function should be outwardly similar. The likeness of form enables the

reader to recognize more readily the likeness of content and function. (http://
sut1.sut.ac.th/strunk/15)

That is, the title of each story ranges from the character's name and a de-
scriptor, as in *Slovenly Peter*, to titles that begin; *The* [adjective] **Dreadful**
Story of . . . , to titles that begin with *The* [adjective] *Story of . . .* and end with
. . . Who Played with Matches, or *Who Would Not Eat Any Soup*. Later titles
seem to belong to a series of their own: *Tom the Thief* and *Frank the Liar*, for
example. Other titles, such as *Cruel Paul*, *Envious Minny*, and *Idle Fritz* can
be grouped according to title format as well. The stories become almost in-
congruous as compared to the original titles.

Because of the way each story evolves through title, text, and illustrations,
it appears as though Hoffmann thought up each successive story as he wrote
them, rather than visualizing the book in its entirety, and did not bother to
revisit the work to make the necessary changes that would tie the collection
together as a cohesive anthology. The text of the first story, *Struwwelpeter*, is
completed in one stanza, while subsequent stories are much lengthier. The
one stanza nursery rhyme evolves over time into drawn out narratives that
are four to five pages in length. This may be evidence in support of the argument that the book was not written in one burst of energy—as a Christmas gift for Hoffmann's son, but that it was pieced together form existing illustrations that Hoffmann produced, over time, for his young patients.

Both the format and design of the illustrations change from beginning to
end as well. *Slovenly Peter*, the first story in the collection, is afforded one illustration, that of the main character, in a head-on full frontal *pose*. This
posed format differs to a great extent from subsequent illustrations that feature multiple vignettes, or scenes containing more than one character, and
also depict action. The illustrations evolve further when decorative borders
and even representational picture frames appear around the vignettes. The
changing format begins to make sense when we consider that Hoffmann
wrote the collection for the sole enjoyment of his own child, not intending,
initially, to publish the work. It does not, however, explain why, upon publication, the collection was not edited for a more consistent format. It seems
that it was the editor, in fact, that changed the format to something less har-
monious.

The content of Hoffmann's *Struwwelpeter* stories are also somewhat in-
consistent. The title, *Struwwelpeter*, or *Slovenly Peter*, indicates that each
story will likely be about one or another childhood behavior, perceived to be
improper, which the majority of the stories are indeed about. Slovenly Peter
neglects to practice proper hygiene, Cruel Frederick teases animals, Pauline

plays with matches, Conrad sucks his thumb, Augustus is a finicky eater, Phillip is fidgety, Johnny is inattentive, and Robert disregards inclement weather and goes outdoors despite the rain. Incidentally, both Phillip and Johnny would likely be diagnosed with an attention deficit disorder today. Nevertheless, all of these children disobey or disregard the rules of proper social behavior and suffer the dire consequences. Each story graphically details the outcome of the child's actions in no uncertain terms.

However, *The Story of the Wild Huntsman* differs from the others in the collection in that this is quite possibly the only story in the collection in which humor is present. This tale is based on the *world turned upside-down* motif wherein the hunter becomes the hunted. No one is killed or even harmed because the nearsighted hare misses her mark, hitting the teacup that the hunter's wife is holding, as she observes the absurd scene unfold from her place in the background.

The story appears to be out of place amid tales of burning girls and amputated thumbs, but is actually the *only* story that is congruent with *Struwwelpeter*'s various subtitles that connote humor in one form or another, such as *Pleasant Stories and Funny Pictures*.

What follows are the ten *Struwwelpeter* stories that appeared in the earliest publications of the book. Beginning with the *Foreword*, we quickly recognize the didactic nature of the text, as well as the intended audience: middle class Christian children. Children who are not *good*, as Hoffmann describes the term *good*, will receive no Christmas gift.

> FOREWORD
> When children have been good,
> That is, be it understood,
> Good at meal-times, good at play,
> Good at night, and good all day,
> They shall have the pretty things
> Merry Christmas always brings.
> Naughty, romping girls and boys
> Tear their clothes and make a noise,
> Soil their aprons and their frocks,
> And deserve no Christmas box.
> Such as these shall never look
> At this pretty Picture Book.

1. SLOVENLY PETER:

See Slovenly Peter! Here he stands, with his dirty hair and hands.
See! His nails are never cut; they are grim'd as black as soot;

No water for many weeks, has been near his cheeks;
And the sloven, I declare, not once this year has combed his hair!
Anything to me is sweeter than to see shock-headed Peter.

2. THE STORY OF CRUEL FREDERICK:

This Frederick! This Frederick! A naughty, wicked boy was he;
He caught the flies, poor little things, and then tore off their tiny wings;
He kill'd the birds, and broke the chairs, and threw the kitten down the stairs;
And oh! far worse and worse, He whipp'd his good and gentle nurse!
The trough was full, and faithful Tray came out to drink one sultry day;
He wagg'd his tail, and wet his lip, when cruel Fred snatch'd up a whip,
And whipp'd poor Tray till he was sore, And kick'd and whipp'd him more and more;
At this, good Tray grow very red, and growl'd and bit him till he bled;
Then you should only have been by, to see how Fred did scream and cry!
So Frederick had to go to bed; His leg was very sore and red! The doctor came and shook his head,
And made a very great to-do, And gave him bitter physic too.
But good dog Tray is happy now; he has no time to say "bow-wow!"
He seats himself in Frederick's chair, and laughs to see the nice things there;
And eats the pies and puddings up.

3. THE DREADFUL STORY OF PAULINE AND THE MATCHES:

Mamma and Nurse went out one day, And left Pauline alone at play;
Around the room she gayly sprung, clapp'd her hands, and danced, and sung,
Now, on the table close at hand, a box of matches chanced to stand,
And kind Mamma and Nurse had told her, That if she touched them they would scold her;
But Pauline said, "Oh, what a pity! For, when they burn, it is so pretty;
They crackle so, and spit, and flame; and Mamma often burns the same.
I'll just light a match or two, as I have often seen my mother do.
When Minz and Maunz, the pussy-cats, heard this they held up their paws and began to hiss.
"Meow!!" they said, "me-ow, me-o! You'll burn to death, if you do so,
Your parents have forbidden you, you know."
But Pauline would not take advice, She lit a match, it was so nice!
It crackled so, it burned so clear, exactly like the picture here.
She jumped for joy and ran about, and was too pleased to put it out.
When Minz and Maunz, the little cats, saw this they said, "Oh, naughty, naughty Miss!" And stretched their claws, And raised their paws;
"Tis very, very wrong, you know; Me-ow, me-o, me-ow, me-o!

You will be burnt if you do so, our mother has forbidden you, you know."
Now see! Oh see, what a dreadful thing, the fire has caught her apron-string;
Her apron burns, her arms, her hair; she burns all over, everywhere.
Then how the pussy-cats did mew, what else, poor pussies, could they do?
They screamed for help, 'twas all in vain, So then, they said, "We'll scream
again.
Make haste, make haste! me-ow! me-o! She'll burn to death, we told her so."
So she was burnt with all her clothes, and arms and hands, and eyes and nose;
Till she had nothing more to lose except her little scarlet shoes;
And nothing else but these was found Among her ashes on the ground.
And when the good cats sat beside the smoking ashes, how they cried!
"Me-ow me-o! ! Me-ow, me-oo! ! What will Mamma and Nursy do?"
Their tears ran down their cheeks so fast. They made a little pond at last.

4. THE STORY OF THE INKY BOYS:

As he had often done before, the woolly-headed black-a-moor
One nice fine summer's day went out to see the shops and walk about;
And as he found it hot, poor fellow, he took with him his green umbrella
Then Edward, little noisy wag, ran out and laugh'd, and waved his flag,
And William came in jacket trim, and brought his wooden hoop with him;
And Caspar, too, snatch'd up his toys and joined the other naughty boys;
So one and all set up a roar, and laughed and hooted more and more,
And kept on singing, only think! "Oh Blacky, you're as black as ink"
Now Saint Nicholas lived close by, so tall he almost touched the sky;
He had a mighty inkstand too, in which a great goose feather grew;
He call'd out in an angry tone, "Boys, leave the black-a-moor alone!
For if he tries with all his might, he cannot change from black to white."
But ah! they did not mind a bit what Saint Nicholas said of it;
But went on laughing, as before, and hooting at the black-a-moor.
Then Saint Nicholas foams with rage: look at him on this very page!
He seizes Caspar, seizes Ned, takes William by his little head;
And they may scream, and kick, and call, But into the ink he dips them all;
Into the inkstand, one, two, three, till they are black, as black can be;
Turn over now and you shall see.
See, there they are, and there they run! The black-a-moor enjoys the fun.
They have been made as black as crows, quite black all over, eyes and nose,
And legs, and arms, and heads, and toes.
And trowsers, pinafores, and toys, the silly little inky boys!
Because they set up such a roar, and teas'd the harmless black-a-moor.

5. THE STORY OF THE WILD HUNTSMAN:

This is the Wild Huntsman that shoots the hares.
With the grass-green coat he always wears.

With game-bag, powder-horn and gun,
He's going out to have some fun.
He finds it hard, without a pair of spectacles, to shoot the hare.
He put his spectacles upon his nose, and said,
"Now I will shoot the hares, and kill them dead."
The hare sits snug in leaves and grass, and laughs to see the green man pass.
Now, as the sun grew very hot, and he a heavy gun had got,
He lay down underneath a tree, and went to sleep, as you may see.
And, while he slept like any top, the little hare came, hop, hop, hop,
n' Took gun and spectacles, and then Softly on tiptoe went off again.
The green man wakes, and sees her place, the spectacles upon her face.
She pointed the gun at the hunter's heart, who jumped up at once with a start.
He cries, and screams, and runs away, "Help me, good people, help! I pray."
At last he stumbled at the well, head over ears, and in he fell.
The hare stopp'd short, took aim, and hark! Bang went the gun!—she miss'd her mark!
The poor man's wife was drinking up, her coffee in her coffee-cup;
The gun shot cup and saucer through; "O dear!" cried she, "what shall I do?"
Hiding, close by the cottage there, was the hare's own child, the little hare;
When he heard the shot, he quickly arose, and while he stood upon his toes,
The coffee fell and burn'd his nose; "O dear," he cried, "what burns me so?"
And held up the spoon with his little toe.

6. THE STORY OF LITTLE SUCK-A-THUMB:

One day, Mamma said, "Conrad dear, I must go out and leave you here.
But mind now, Conrad, what I say, don't suck your thumb while I'm away.
The great tall tailor always comes to little boys that suck their thumbs.
And ere they dream what he's about he takes his great sharp scissors out
And cuts their thumbs clean off, —and then you know, they never grow again."
Mamma had scarcely turn'd her back, the thumb was in, alack! alack!
The door flew open, in he ran, the great, long, red-legged scissorman.
Oh! Children, see! The tailor's come and caught our little Suck-a-Thumb.
Snip! Snap! Snip! the scissors go; and Conrad cries out—Oh! Oh! Oh!
Snip! Snap! Snip! They go so fast; that both his thumbs are off at last.
Mamma comes home; there Conrad stands, and looks quite sad, and shows his hands; "Ah!" said Mamma "I knew he'd come to naughty little Suck-a-Thumb."

7. THE STORY OF AUGUSTUS
WHO WOULD NOT HAVE ANY SOUP:

Augustus was a chubby lad; Fat ruddy cheeks Augustus had;
And everybody saw with joy the plump and hearty healthy boy.

He ate and drank as he was told, and never let his soup get cold.
But one day, one cold winter's day, he threw away the spoon and screamed:
"O take the nasty soup away! I won't have any soup to-day:
I will not, will not eat my soup! I will not eat it, no!"
Next day! Now look, the picture shows how lank and lean Augustus grows!
Yet, though he feels so weak and ill, the naughty fellow cries out still.
"Not any soup for me, I say! O take the nasty soup away!
I will not, will not eat my soup! I will not eat it, no!"
The third day comes. O what a sin! To make himself so pale and thin.
Yet, when the soup is put on table, he screams, as loud as he is able
"Not any soup for me, I say! O take the nasty soup away! I won't have any
soup to-day!"
Look at him, now the fourth day's come! He scarce outweighs a sugar-plum;
He's like a little bit of thread; and on the fifth day he was dead.

8. THE STORY OF FIDGETY PHILIP:

"Let me see if Philip can be a little gentleman;
Let me see if he is able to sit still for once at table."
Thus spoke, in earnest tone, the father to his son;
And the mother looked very grave to see Philip so misbehave.
But Philip he did not mind his father who was so kind.
He wriggled, and giggled, and then, I declare,
Swung backward and forward and tilted his chair,
Just like any rocking horse; "Philip! I am getting cross!"
See the naughty, restless child, growing still more rude and wild,
Till his chair falls over quite. Philip screams with all his might,
Catches at the cloth, but then that makes matters worse again.
Down upon the ground they fall, glasses, bread, knives forks and all.
How Mamma did fret and frown, when she saw them tumbling down!
And Papa made such a face! Philip is in sad disgrace.
Where is Philip? Where is he? Fairly cover'd up, you see!
Cloth and all are lying on him; he has pull'd down all upon him!
What a terrible to-do! Dishes, glasses, snap't in two!
Here a knife, and there a fork! Philip, this is naughty work.
Table all so bare, and ah! Poor Papa and poor Mamma Look quite cross,
and wonder how They shall make their dinner now.

9. THE STORY OF JOHNNY LOOK-IN-THE-AIR:

As he trudg'd along to school, it was always Johnny's rule
To be looking at the sky and the clouds that floated by;
But what just before him lay, in his way,
Johnny never thought about; So that every one cried out,
"Look at little Johnny there, Little Johnny Head-In-Air!"

Running just in Johnny's way, came a little dog one day; Johnny's eyes were still astray

Up on high, in the sky; and he never heard them cry—"Johnny, mind, the dog is nigh!" What happens now? Bump! Dump! Down they fell, with such a thump, dog and Johnny in a lump!

They almost broke their bones, so hard they tumbled on the stones.

Once, with head as high as ever, Johnny walked beside the river.

Johnny watch'd the swallows trying which was cleverest at flying.

Oh! what fun! Johnny watch'd the bright round sun

Going in and coming out; this was all he thought about.

So he strode on, only think! To the river's very brink,

Where the bank was high and steep, and the water very deep;

And the fishes, in a row, stared to see him coming so.

One step more! Oh! sad to tell! Headlong in poor Johnny fell.

The three little fishes, in dismay, wagged their tails and swam away.

There lay Johnny on his face; with his nice red writing-case;

But, as they were passing by, two strong men had heard him cry;

And, with sticks, these two strong men hook'd poor Johnny out again.

Oh! you should have seen him shiver when they pull'd him from the river.

He was in a sorry plight, dripping wet, and such a fright!

Wet all over, everywhere, clothes, and arms, and face, and hair.

Johnny never will forget what it is to be so wet.

And the fishes, one, two, three, are come back again, you see;

Up they came the moment after, to enjoy the fun and laughter.

Each popp'd out his little head, and, to tease poor Johnny, said,

"Silly little Johnny, look, you have lost your writing-book!"

Look at them laughing and do you see? His satchel is drifting, far out to sea!

10. THE STORY OF FLYING ROBERT:

When the rain comes tumbling down in the country or the town,

All good little girls and boys stay at home and mind their toys.

Robert thought, —"No, when it pours, It is better out of doors."

Rain it did, and in a minute Rob was in it.

Here you see him, silly fellow, underneath his red umbrella.

What a wind! Oh! How it whistles Through the trees and flow'rs and thistles.

It has caught his red umbrella; Now look at him, silly fellow,

Up he flies. To the skies. No one heard his screams and cries;

Through the clouds the rude wind bore him, and his hat flew on before him.

Soon they got to such height, they were nearly out of sight!

And the hat went up so high, that it almost touch'd the sky.

No one ever yet could tell where they stopp'd, or where they fell;

Only this one thing is plain, Rob was never seen again!

CHAPTER FIVE

Parodies, Spin-Offs, and Other Nineteenth Century Children's Stories

The Parodies

Parody is defined in the dictionary as a musical or literary work that imitates another work, exaggerating the characteristics of the original to make it seem ridiculous. More specifically though, a work can be called a parody when we take a readily recognizable existing work's format, and imbed into that work a new concept. A work is only parodied then, if it is clearly recognizable, as in a classic, or perhaps a pop culture phenomenon. If the work to be parodied is unfamiliar then the meaning is lost and hence the intent. Parodies are typically satirical in their imitation and often they are politically driven, but can also be sentimental and used to poke affectionate fun at the original work. *Struwwelpeter* is a significant literary work that has become so widely recognized that it merits parodies, retellings, translations, adaptations, imitations, and inspiration for a junk opera as well as board games, children's books with cassettes or CDs, 33 rpm record albums, puppets, posters, wooden toy characters, coffee cups, paper napkins, and other paraphernalia. There is even a *Struwwelpeter Museum* located at der Schirn Kunsthalle Römerberg, Bendergasse 1, 60311 Frankfurt, Germany, and images from the *Struwwelpeter* stories are so familiar in Germany that they appear in advertising and as park statuary. The *Struwwelpeter* book, originally an inauspicious project with an unremarkable publication, has unexpectedly developed into a worldwide infamous hit.

Folkloric scholars too have expressed their interest in *Der Struwwelpeter* with articles, journals, and academic conferences dedicated to the analysis of these intriguing stories. *Struwwelpeter Revisited* was an international symposium held at the University of Minnesota in November of 1995. Directed by Gerhard Weiss, Department Chair of German, this conference paid homage to the German children's classic with presentations by international scholars such as the paper presented by Adelheid Hlawacek titled, *The Egyptian Struwwelpeter, a Curiosity in Austria's Juvenile Literature?*

The *Egyptian Struwwelpeter* was actually written in Austria by siblings Richard, Fritz, and Magdelene Netolitzky, simply because Egyptian art, artifacts, and culture were popular in Austria, as were the *Struwwelpeter* stories in the late nineteenth century. It is a rare book with only a handful remaining in libraries, museums, and private collections. The title story features *Thoth the Inky Boy*, a hybrid of *Slovenly Peter* and *The Inky Boys*. Thoth was the Egyptian moon god, the inventor of spoken and written language, the lord of books, and the patron of all scribes. In the title story, *Thoth the Inky Boy*, Thoth is posed on a pedestal, like Peter, but instead of being "shock-headed," he is splattered with ink stains. Dressed as a traditional Egyptian scribe and holding papyrus and rush, Thoth is surrounded by hieroglyphs and palm trees. His greatest joy is splashing in ink.

A subsequent conference titled *Struwwelpeter in English: Contemporaries and Successors* was held at Princeton University to celebrate the 150th anniversary of the publication of the first *Struwwelpeter* book, where an audience of children's book scholars and collectors listened to thirteen speakers from the United States, Britain, and Germany present their papers on *Struwwelpeter*. These conferences testify to the enormous impact that *Struwwelpeter* has had on nineteenth century children's literature.

Most of the parodies and adaptations are sophisticated works aimed at an adult audience who is assumed to be well acquainted with the original work. One of the earliest adaptations is assumed to be *The Political Struwwelpeter*, written by Edward Harold Begbie and published in London in 1899. Here the sloven is the neglected British lion which satirizes the political climate of the time. Begbie also published the *Struwwelpeter Alphabet* in 1900 which depicts British royalty, among other important figures, in unflattering ways (Weiss, G., 1996). Gerhard Weiss offers a comprehensive list of parodies in his article published in *The Lion and the Unicorn* (Dec. 1996) including *Grober Struwwelpeter* by Richard Schmidt-Cabanis (1877), *Swollen-Headed William* by Edward Lucas (1914), and *Truffel Eater: Pretty Stories and Funny Pictures* by Oistros (pseudonym meaning *Horse Fly*) (1933); all based on the *Struwwelpeter* theme.

However, *Struwwelhitler* and *Tricky Dick and His Pals* are two of the more well known parodies of *Struwwelpeter*. Both are political satire aimed at world leaders: Adolph Hitler and Richard Nixon. *Struwwelhitler* is a WWII era British parody of *Struwwelpeter* written by Robert and Philip Spence and presented to the *Daily Sketch War Relief Fund* in England. A caricature of Adolph Hitler replaces Slovenly Peter on the book's cover. Hitler's hair is a tangled mass and his fingers spurt blood. He is posed on a pedestal, in the same stance as Slovenly Peter, with a look of chagrin on his face. The inscription on the pedestal reads:

> Just look at him! There he stands, with his nasty hair and hands.
> See! The horrid blood drops drip, from each dirty finger tip;
> And the sloven, I declare, never once has combed his hair;
> Piecrust never could be brittler than the word of Adolph Hitler.

Each of the stories that follow parody one of the *Struwwelpeter* stories, with Hitler and the Nazi party featured as the main characters. Lines such as these, in *Cruel Adolph*, leave no doubt in the reader's mind of the intentional anti-Nazi sentiment:

> When patient Fritz in abject mood, complained that he was short of food,
> "Be off!" cried Adolph, "Greedy scamp! To Dachau Concentration Camp."

Tricky Dick and His Pals follows the same format as *Struwwelpeter* and *Struwwelhitler*, this time with a caricature of Richard Millhouse Nixon on the front cover. Written by Dr. Joseph Wortis and published in 1974, this story admonishes President Nixon and his Administration. Richard Nixon is posed as Slovenly Peter on the cover, but with his arms raised in the air rather than hanging at his sides. He is giving the audience his signature gesture: his hands clenched in fists with his index and middle fingers raised, a motion that may be interpreted either as the victory sign popular after WWII, or as the peace sign popular during the Nixon Administration.

Instead of the pedestal on which Slovenly Peter stands, Nixon is posed on a dog house. The opening story reads, in part:

> Look at this child so clean and slick, He's called Obnoxious Tricky Dick!
> He'd lie and cheat and hit and steal, and wouldn't care how bad you feel.

What follows are stories that parody the Nixon Administration more so than the *Struwwelpeter* stories, with titles such as *Dick the Snooper* and *Dick Goes Shopping*. However, in *Uncle Sam's Illness*, Wortis vaguely incorporates some of the *Struwwelpter* motifs when Dicky gets bitten by a dog (Cruel Frederick) and shoots himself with his own gun (The Wild Huntsman). Wortis also makes some amusing references to Nixon's Vice President and to his cabinet members. As an example, in *The Nasty Tongue* story, we read about *Kid Spagno* who "made each kid pay off a dime, and then he tried to hide his crime" (Wortis, 1974). As well, there is a reference to the *Katzenjammer Kids* who were inspired by the *Max and Moritz* tales, popular about the time of the publication of *Struwwelpeter*.

One of the more bizarre parodies is *Shockheaded Peter: A Junk Opera* which is performed by The Tiger Lillies, a three piece band with a large cult following in London. Their interpretation of *Struwwelpeter* is a chilling rendition of Hoffmann's stories taken to their most violent extremes. The audience is left somewhat unnerved by the experience of watching the production. In this performance *The Inky Boys* are replaced by *The Bully Boys* who ultimately have their heads smashed to bits for being annoying. As well, Conrad, whose thumbs are amputated in the Hoffmann version of *Little Suck-A-Thumb*, bleeds to death in The Tiger Lillies's version. And *The Story of The Wild Huntsman*, which is among the least violent of Hoffmann's stories, becomes disturbingly cruel and brutal in the theatrical production. While Hoffmann depicted a somewhat humorous version of the tale with the hare pointing her gun at the hunter, pulling the trigger, missing her mark, and hitting instead the teacup held by the hunter's wife, The Tiger Lillies depict a crueler scenario. In their interpretation of the same story the hare stalks and then murders the huntsman *and* his wife. She then kills her own offspring and finally turns the gun on herself to commit suicide in an alarming triple homicide/suicide.

A more recent, and only slightly less violent retelling of Hoffmann's *Struwwelpeter* is Bob Staake's version wherein he facetiously states that his 2006 adaptation remains faithful to the original, "all inappropriateness, Teutonic didacticism, and political incorrectness firmly intact." While I agree with Slaake's assessment I would have worded it a bit differently. In particular, I would not credit the didacticism with being solely Tuetonic in nature. Didacticism was more widespread than that. And as for being inappropriate, I do agree that it is *developmentally* inappropriate for the original targeted audience of three-year-olds. I feel that the distinction between inappropriateness and developmental inappropriateness is an important one, and almost no subject matter is off limits provided it is delivered in a developmentally appropriate manner. Finally, the political incorrectness which Staake refers to is probably most obvious in *The Inky Boys* story which uses phrases like "wooly-headed black-a-moor" to describe the African character. However, I feel that this story transcends the somewhat superficial *politically incorrect* label and enters into the realm of overt racism.

Of course, Staake's adaptation would not be as good as it is had he deviated too far from the original by whitewashing the story, as has befallen many of the Grimms' tales. Staake's unique rendition combines a cutting edge contemporary aesthetic with irreverently humorous text that remains surprisingly true to the original.

Peter is slovenly as ever in this latest version with his wildly unkempt hair, impossibly long fingernails, and dirty clothing, but Staake takes Peter's disgraceful state a step further by adding the element of stench to Peter's overall comportment. Peter's scent is compared to "poop" and "puke." He is described as "gross" with a most ghastly unpleasant aroma of "lethal dose" proportions. The rhyme scheme—*gross* with *dose* and *whiff* with *sniff*—is irreverently humorous and scandalously appealing to juvenile readers who are taught that such language (poop) is inappropriate in certain *proper* social settings.

It is this element of irreverence that catapults the story into the twenty-first century—fully separating it from a strict didactic tradition of imparting proper social behaviors—ready to entertain and frighten yet another generation of young and old readers alike.

Competition

The immense popularity of Hoffmann's *Struwwelpeter* triggered intense competition in the children's book market. Noting the popularity of the original, and because *Struwwelpeter* featured boys in all but one of the stories, publishers and authors alike scrambled to fill the void by writing similar stories about naughty girls. Many were blatant imitations of Hoffmann's work with titles like *The Girl Who Would Not Comb Her Hair* and *The Dreadful Story of the Girl and the Lucifer Matches*. Other authors added *Struwwel* to the title of their books about naughty girls which insured consumers that they were getting the same popular stories that they were already so familiar with. *Struwwelsuse*, *Struwwellieses*, *Struwwelhanne*, *Struwwel-Lene*, and *Struwwelpetra* are a few. As a collection, these female cautionary tales are sometimes called *Mädchenstruwwelpeteriades* (Wiedmann, 2000).

Slovenly Betsy, an Americanized version of *Slovenly Peter*, is one of the most recognizable of the female cautionary tales. Written by a "Henry Hoffmann" and originally published in 1911, these moralistic tales warn girls of what befalls them when they misbehave. Our protagonist, Betsy, is a girl who neglects to bathe or comb her hair and the schoolboys all poke fun at her disheveled appearance. One day Betsy's parents dress her in clean clothes and take her to visit family friends where Betsy promptly finds a mud puddle. She falls in, becomes covered with mud, and tears her dress. Upon seeing this, the guests laugh at her. The text reads, "She almost died with shame." She turns and runs home then, "She washed her clothes and since has been as neat as she could be" (Hoffmann, 1995).

The story line makes little sense, of course, as it lacks internal logic. Why did she not care when the schoolboys teased her, but almost *died of shame* when children at the house of her parents' friends teased her? Did she really make such a dramatic turnaround in her personality and grooming habits because of one incident? Internal logic aside, this is a cautionary tale and little attention is paid to literary quality.

Further competition came in the form of imitations and spin-offs and the last four decades of the nineteenth century saw a wave of *Struwwelpeter* inspired cautionary tales published in New York by McLoughlin Bros. Many of these tales were translations of the originals in German, some by Heinrich Hoffmann, some by recognized German authors, and others by unknown authors. Their *Slovenly Peter* series featured *Slovenly Peter's Little Story Books* which contained American versions of several of Heinrich Hoffmann's stories as well as other *Struwwelpeter* inspired cautionary tales such as *Envious Minnie*, *The Little Glutton*, *Tom the Thief*, and *The Dirty Child*.

As well, McLoughlin Bros. published the *Aunt Oddamadodd* series, the *Aunt Grumbles* series, and the *Aunt Lulu* series which all featured variations of the original *Struwwelpeter* stories plus American cautionary tales of the same ilk, many of which were pirated from the German originals.

Max and Moritz

Of all the nineteenth century German children's stories, it is the story of *Max and Moritz* that is most frequently seen paired with *Struwwelpeter*, often as a dual publication of the two stories, several of which are still in print. Max and Moritz are wayward boys that get themselves into a variety of unpleasant situations ranging in severity from mischievous to malicious, such as stealing apples or hanging chickens from a tree. They are the inspiration for the famous Rudolph Dirks comic strip, *The Katzenjammer Kids*, created in 1897. *The Katzenjammer Kids* featured the impish twins, Hans and Fritz, who rebelled against all forms of authority including Mama, der Captain, and der Inspector. Max and Moritz who wreak havoc in their town are eventually done in when they are ground up in the flour mill, thereby freeing the town from their "rascality."

Following the untimely death of Max and Moritz the townsfolk speak in hushed whispers: "Widow Tibbetts speaking low, said 'I thought it would be so.'" Uncle adds his commentary as well, "See what comes of stupid jokes," he says of their untimely deaths. Crime does not pay for these mischievous boys whose pulverized remains are gobbled up by Master Miller's hungry ducks in the coarse-grained feed that is comprised of their "postmortem bits."

Max and Moritz: A Juvenile History in Seven Tricks by Wilhelm Busch

FOREWORD

Ah, how oft we read or hear of, boys we almost stand in fear of!
For example, take these stories of two youths, named Max and Moritz,
Who, instead of early turning their young minds to useful learning,
Often leered with horrid features at their lessons and their teachers.
Look now at the empty head: he is for mischief always ready.
Teasing creatures—climbing fences, stealing apples, pears, and quinces,
Is, of course, a deal more pleasant, and far easier for the present,
Than to sit in schools or churches, fixed like roosters on their perches
But O dear, O dear, O deary, when the end comes sad and dreary!
'Tis a dreadful thing to tell that on Max and Moritz fell!
All they did this book rehearses, both in pictures and in verses.

FIRST TRICK

To most people who have leisure raising poultry gives great pleasure:
First, because the eggs they lay us, for the care we take repay us;
Secondly, that now and then we can dine on roasted hen;
Thirdly, of the hen's and goose's feathers men make various uses.
Some folks like to rest their heads in the night on feather beds.
One of these was Widow Tibbets, whom the cut you see exhibits.
Hens were hers in number three, and a cock of majesty.
Max and Moritz took a view; fell to thinking what to do.
One, two, three! as soon as said, they have sliced a loaf of bread,
Cut each piece again in four, each a finger thick, no more.
These to two cross-threads they tie, like a letter X they lie
In the widow's yard, with care stretched by those two rascals there.
Scarce the cock had seen the sight, when he up and crew with might:
Cock-a-doodle-doodle-doo; —Tack, tack, tack, the trio flew.
Cock and hens, like fowls unfed, gobbled each a piece of bread;
But they found, on taking thought, each of them was badly caught.
Every way they pull and twitch, this strange cat's-cradle to unhitch;
Up into the air they fly, Jiminee, O Jimini!
On a tree behold them dangling, in the agony of strangling!

And their necks grow long and longer, and their groans grow strong and stronger.
Each lays quickly one egg more, then they cross to th' other shore.
Widow Tibbets in her chamber, by these death-cries waked from slumber,
Rushes out with bodeful thought: Heavens! What sight her vision caught!
From her eyes the tears are streaming: "Oh, my cares, my toil, my dreaming!
Ah, life's fairest hope," says she, "Hangs upon that apple-tree."
Heart-sick (you may well suppose), for the carving-knife she goes;
Cuts the bodies from the bough, hanging cold and lifeless now;
And in silence, bathed in tears, through her house-door disappears.
This was the bad boys' first trick, but the second follows quick.

SECOND TRICK

When the worthy Widow Tibbets (Whom the cut below exhibits)
Had recovered, on the morrow, From the dreadful shock of sorrow,
She (as soon as grief would let her Think) began to think 'twere better
Just to take the dead, the dear ones (Who in life were walking here once),
And in a still noonday hour them, well roasted, to devour.
True, it did seem almost wicked, when they lay so bare and naked,
Picked, and singed before the blaze, —they that once in happier days,
In the yard or garden ground, all day long went scratching round.
Ah ! Frau Tibbets wept anew, and poor Spitz was with her, too.
Max and Moritz smelt the savor. "Climb the roof!" cried each young shaver.
Through the chimney now, with pleasure, they behold the tempting treasure,
Headless, in the pan there, lying, hissing, browning, steaming, frying.
At that moment down the cellar (Dreaming not what soon befell her)
Widow Tibbets went for sour krout, which she would oft devour
With exceeding great desire (Warmed a little at the fire).
Up there on the roof, meanwhile, they are doing things in style.
Max already with forethought a long fishing-line has brought.
Schnupdiwup! a second bird! Schnupdiwup! up comes the third!
Presto! number four they haul! Schnupdiwup! we have them all!—
Spitz looks on, we must allow, but he barks: Row-wow! Row-wow!
But the rogues are down instantly from the roof, and off they canter.
Ha! I guess there'll be a humming; here's the Widow Tibbets coming!
Rooted stood she to the spot, when the pan her vision caught.
Gone was every blessed bird! "Horrid Spitz!" was her first word.
"O you Spitz, you monster, you! Let me beat him black and blue!"
And the heavy ladle, thwack! Comes down on poor Spitz's back!
Loud he yells with agony, for he feels his conscience free.
Max and Moritz, dinner over, in a hedge, snored under cover;
And of that great hen-feast now each has but a leg to show.
This was now the second trick, but the third will follow quick.

THIRD TRICK

Through the town and country round was one Mr. Buck renowned.
Sunday coats, and week-day sackcoats, bob-tails, swallow-tails, and frock coats,
Gaiters, breeches, hunting-jackets; waistcoats, with commodious pockets,—
And other things, too long to mention, claimed Mr. Tailor Buck's attention.
Or, if any thing wanted doing in the way of darning, sewing,
Piecing, patching, —if a button needed to be fixed or put on,—
Any thing of any kind, anywhere, before, behind,—
Master Buck could do the same, for it was his life's great aim.
Therefore all the population held him high in estimation.
Max and Moritz tried to invent ways to plague this worthy gent.
Right before the Sartor's dwelling ran a swift stream, roaring, swelling.
This swift stream a bridge did span. And the road across it ran.
Max and Moritz (naught could awe them!) Took a saw, when no one saw them:
Ritze-ratze ! riddle-diddle! Sawed a gap across the middle.
When this feat was finished well, suddenly was heard a yell:
"Hallo, there! Come out, you buck! Tailor, Tailor, muck! muck! muck!"
Buck could bear all sorts of jeering, jibes and jokes in silence hearing;
But this insult roused such anger, nature couldn't stand it longer.
Wild with fury, up he started, with his yard-stick out he darted;
For once more that frightful jeer, "Muck! muck! muck!" rang loud and clear.
On the bridge one leap he makes; crash! beneath his weight it breaks.
Once more rings the cry, "Muck! muck!" In, headforemost, plumps poor Buck!
While the scared boys were skedaddling, down the brook two geese came paddling.
On the legs of these two geese, with a death-clutch, Buck did seize;
And, with both geese well in hand, flutters out upon dry land.
For the rest he did not find things exactly to his mind.
Soon it proved poor Buck had brought a dreadful belly-ache from the water.
Noble Mrs. Buck! She rises fully equal to the crisis;
With a hot flat-iron, she draws the cold out famously.
Soon 'twas in the mouths of men, all through town: "Buck's up again!"
This was the bad boys' third trick, but the fourth will follow quick.

FOURTH TRICK

An old saw runs somewhat so: man must learn while here below
Not alone the A, B, C, raises man in dignity;
Not alone in reading, writing, reason finds a work inviting;
Not alone to solve the double rule of Three shall man take trouble;

But must hear with pleasure Sages teach the wisdom of the ages.
Of this wisdom an example to the world was Master Sampel.
For this cause, to Max and Moritz this man was the chief of horrors;
For a boy who loves bad tricks wisdom's friendship never seeks.
With the clerical profession smoking always was a passion;
And this habit without question, while it helps promote digestion,
Is a comfort no one can well begrudge a good old man,
When the day's vexations close, and he sits to seek repose.
Max and Moritz, flinty-hearted, on another trick have started;
Thinking how they may attack a poor old man through his tobacco.
Once, when Sunday morning breaking, pious hearts to gladness waking,
Poured its light where, in the temple, at his organ sat Herr Sampel,
These bad boys, for mischief ready, stole into the good man's study,
Where his darling meerschaum stands. This, Max holds in both his hands;
While young Moritz (scapegrace born!) Climbs, and gets the powderhorn,
And with speed the wicked soul pours the powder in the bowl.
Hush, and quick! now, right about! For already church is out.
Sampel closes the church-door glad to seek his home once more;
All his service well got through, takes his keys, and music too,
And his way, delighted, wends homeward to his silent friends.
Full of gratitude he there lights his pipe, and takes his chair.
"Ah!" he says, "no joy is found like contentment on earth's round!"
Fizz! whizz! bum! The pipe is burst, almost shattered into dust.
Coffee-pot and water-jug, snuff-box, ink-stand, tumbler, mug,
Table, stove, and easy-chair, all are flying through the air
In a lightning-powder-flash, with a most tremendous crash.
When the smoke-cloud lifts and clears, Sampel on his back appears;
God be praised! still breathing there, only somewhat worse for wear.
Nose, hands, eyebrows (once like yours), now are black as any Moor's;
Burned the last thin spear of hair, and his pate is wholly bare.
Who shall now the children guide, lead their steps to wisdom's side?
Who shall now for Master Sampel lead the service in the temple?
Now that his old pipe is out, shattered, smashed, gone up the spout?
Time will heal the rest once more, but the pipe's best days are o'er.
This was the bad boys' fourth trick, but the fifth will follow quick.

FIFTH TRICK

If, in village or in town, you've an uncle settled down,
Always treat him courteously; Uncle will be pleased thereby.
In the morning: "Morning to you! Any errand I can do you?"
Fetch whatever he may need, —pipe to smoke, and news to read;
Or should some confounded thing prick his back, or bite, or sting,

Nephew then will be near by, ready to his help to fly;
Or a pinch of snuff, maybe, sets him sneezing violently:
"Prosit! uncle! good health to you! God be praised! much good may't do you!"
Or he comes home late, perchance: pull his boots off then at once,
Fetch his slippers and his cap, and warm gown his limbs to wrap.
Be your constant care, good boy, what shall give your uncle joy.
Max and Moritz (need I mention?) Had not any such intention.
See now how they tried their wits—these bad boys—on Uncle Fritz.
What kind of a bird a May bug was, they knew, I dare say;
In the trees they may be found, flying, crawling, wriggling round.
Max and Moritz, great pains taking, from a tree these bugs are shaking.
In their cornucopia papers, they collect these pinching creepers.
Soon they are deposited in the foot of uncle's bed!
With his peaked nightcap on, Uncle Fritz to bed has gone;
Tucks the clothes in, shuts his eyes, and in sweetest slumber lies.
Kritze! Kratze! come the Tartars single file from their night quarters.
And the captain boldly goes straight at Uncle Fritzy's nose.
"Baugh!" he cries: "what have we here?" Seizing that grim grenadier.
Uncle, wild with fright, upspringeth, and the bedclothes from him flingeth.
"Awtsch!" he seizes two more scape graces from his shin and nape.
Crawling, flying, to and fro, round the buzzing rascals go.
Wild with fury, Uncle Fritz stamps and slashes them to bits.
O be joyful! all gone by is the May bug's deviltry.
Uncle Fritz his eyes can close once again in sweet repose.
This was the bad boys' fifth trick, but the sixth will follow quick.

SIXTH TRICK

Easter days have come again, when the pious baker men
Bake all sorts of sugar things, plum-cakes, ginger-cakes, and rings.
Max and Moritz feel an ache in their sweet-tooth for some cake.
But the Baker thoughtfully locks his shop, and takes the key.
Who would steal, then, this must do: wriggle down the chimney-flue.
Ratsch! There come the boys, my Jiminy! Black as ravens, down the
chimney.
Puff! into a chest they drop full of flour up to the top.
Out they crawl from under cover just as white as chalk all over.
But the cracknels, precious treasure, on a shelf they spy with pleasure.
Knacks! The chair breaks! down they go—Schwapp!—into a trough of
dough!
All enveloped now in dough, see them, monuments of woe.
In the Baker comes, and snickers when he sees the sugar-lickers.
One, two, three! the brats, behold! Into two good brots are rolled.

There's the oven, all red-hot,—shove 'em in as quick as thought.
Ruff! out with 'em from the heat, they are brown and good to eat.
Now you think they've paid the debt! No, my friend, they're living yet.
Knusper! Knasper! like two mice through their roofs they gnaw in a trice;
And the Baker cries, "You bet! There's the rascals living yet!"
This was the bad boys' sixth trick, but the last will follow quick.

LAST TRICK

Max and Moritz! I grow sick, when I think on your last trick.
Why must these two scalawags cut those gashes in the bags?
See! the farmer on his back carries corn off in a sack.
Scarce has he begun to travel, when the corn runs out like gravel.
All at once he stops and cries: "Darn it! I see where it lies!"
Ha! With what delighted eyes Max and Moritz he espies.
Rabs! he opens wide his sack, shoves the rogues in—Hukepack!
It grows warm with Max and Moritz, for to mill the farmer hurries.
"Master Miller! Hallo, man! Grind me that as quick as you can!"
"In with 'em!" Each wretched flopper headlong goes into the hopper.
As the farmer turns his back, he hears the mill go "creaky! cracky!"
Here you see the bits post mortem, just as Fate was pleased to sort 'em.
Master Miller's ducks with speed gobbled up the coarse-grained feed.

CONCLUSION

In the village not a word, not a sign, of grief, was heard.
Widow Tibbets speaking low, said, "I thought it would be so!"
"None but self," cried Buck, "to blame! Mischief is not life's true aim!"
Then said gravely Teacher Sampel, "There again is an example!"
"To be sure! bad thing for youth," Said the Baker, "a sweet tooth!"
Even Uncle says, "Good folks! See what comes of stupid jokes!"
But the honest farmer: "Guy! What concern is that to I?"
Through the place in short there went one wide murmur of content:
"God be praised! the town is free from this great rascality!"

CHAPTER SIX

Contemporary Children's Literature and the Absence of Didacticism

Didacticism

While children's literature can be traced back through history to Hornbooks, Chapbooks, and even to the famous *Orbis Sensualium Pictus*, published in 1656 by John Amos Comenius, and considered by many to be the first picture book for children, the contemporary phrase *children's literature* implies something altogether different from the didactic illustrated passages that these publications represent. These early books were little more than moral and/or academic lessons for children to dutifully memorize and live by—or suffer the consequence.

Literature, by definition, is writing of lasting value and excellence, at the heart of which is a distinct focus on plot, characterization, setting, theme, style, and point of view—all of which combine to help the reader to make a personal and meaningful connection to the text. We understand reading to be a dynamic and interactive pastime that is both pleasurable and informational. Children who read good literature are not merely decoding the written words on a page, but are comprehending the meaning—both at the surface level and the underlying truth, or theme, of the written story—and making connections that open up new possibilities and ways of thinking that encourage critical thinking skills.

This is what we call *engaged* reading. According to James Jacobs and Michael Tunnell, "Unengaged reading is the reading of necessity, the reading required by others or forced on us . . . most often reading imposed by work or school remains unengaged, speaking neither to our heads nor to our hearts" (Jacobs and Tunnell, 2004, p. 6).

High quality contemporary children's literature offers the engaged reader a personally meaningful experience that transcends efferent reading, or reading to gain information, rather than reading for pleasure. High quality literature contains intriguing plots, well developed and believable characters, richly described settings that appeal to all five senses, themes that are relevant to the reader audience, and a distinct absence of didacticism. High quality literature does not tell the reader what to think. Rather, it portrays a situation and the intelligent reader can glean their own meaning based on the story's circumstances, as well as the reader's own personal experience and background knowledge. Early children's books lacked such a literary focus. The story line was secondary to the moral lesson, which was stated overtly, with no room for misinterpretation. Literary quality was not a consideration. Characters were underdeveloped and existed only to deliver the message of morality.

Ironically, it was Dr. Hoffmanns' *Struwwelpeter* that was met with unprecedented success for its *absence of didacticism*. These books virtually flew off of bookstore shelves, purchased by adults who were drawn to its supposedly *humorous* pictures and *funny* stories. The widespread appeal was due primarily to the novelty of the book, the likes of which no one had previously seen. However, when compared to today's standards for literary quality, the *Struwwelpeter* stories seem to be the epitome of didacticism: children are instructed to behave well or suffer a swift and severe consequence.

Nevertheless, the distinct didactic nature of these stories differs from earlier children's fare in that *full color* illustrations accompany short *stories*. The format was a significant departure from other children's books and the text—or short story—was dramatically different from a typical passage found in earlier children's books such as *McGuffy's Eclectic Primer* (c. 1836), for example. Lesson IX in the McGuffy primer reads, "I see a tub. The tub is big. Can you use it? Oh yes, I can. I can use it." A wash tub is pictured above the text. Thus, children learn to recognize a wash tub. The text is instructional and linear. It tells no story, nor does it reveal any underlying truth. It does not move us emotionally nor does it touch the human spirit. It merely instructs us to recognize a wash tub. When compared to *McGuffy's Ecelctic Primer*, which was a typical children's book in its day, the *Struwwelpeter* stories appear less didactic than when judged by contemporary standards.

The format of the *Struwwelpeter* stories was novel in that short stories replaced mere instructional lines of text to be memorized by the reader. Imbedded within the *Struwwelpeter* story was the moral or lesson. The reader could infer, for example, that Slovenly Peter should feel ashamed of himself for having extraordinarily poor hygiene, and this notion of inference was credited for elevating the stories from a dull and preachy didactic tradition.

Moreover, the illustrations, rendered in full color, were believed to be humorous in their farcical absurdity; of *course* a tailor would not rush in to snap off Conrad's thumbs and leave him bleeding . . . but does the targeted three-year-old audience understand the absurdity? Apparently their parents recognized the purported farce—based on the astronomical sales of the book—and delighted in the book's humor. However, whether absurdly funny or shockingly violent, the illustrations, depicting burning and bleeding children, would be unlikely choices for contemporary young children's picture books.

Although Hoffmann's *Struwwelpeter* was considered a novelty, both in format and for its supposed absence of didacticism, it was not the first children's book to attempt a break from the didactic tradition. John Newbery's famous children's book titled, *A Little Pretty Pocket-book: Intended for the Instruction and Amusement of Little Master Tommy, and Pretty Miss Polly*, which preceded Heinrich Hoffmann's picture book by one hundred years, was first published in England in 1744. This is considered by many to be the first children's book—although many others credit Comenius and his *Orbitus Sensualium Pictus* as the first *picture* book for children. The question, however, is not who wrote the first children's book, but who was the first to break away from the didactic tradition to write the first engaging and entertaining children's book? The focus of Newbery's book was not solely instructional, but was also intended for the amusement of the reader, as its title indicates. Despite the attempt at entertainment, it still comes across as a heavily didactic primer both aesthetically and in format. Filled with simple rhymes and black and white illustrations of children playing games, it includes lessons on the proper use of everyday artifacts, such as a pincushion.

Newbery's attempt at entertainment is commendable. In theory, Newbery recognized the importance of engagement in the reading process, yet mere pictures of children at play only begin to break the didactic mold and to move toward rich literary quality that truly entertains the reader. While Newbery had taken the first steps toward literary quality, the text remained superficially instructional. Nevertheless Newbery went on to be the first commercial publisher of children's books and the coveted John Newbery Medal is awarded annually to the book that is considered to be the most outstanding work of children's literature.

J. D. Stahl, who wrote *Struwwelpeter and the Development of the American Children's Book*, believes that it was writers such as Mark Twain and Louisa May Alcott, whose "ambivalent or hostile attitudes toward the didactic tradition"

(Stahl, p. 34) shaped America's twentieth century mind-set regarding these horrible cautionary stories. Stahl notes the shopworn binary of didactic versus imaginative writing evidenced in much of the commentary on children's literature, and credits Alcott and Twain, both exceptional writers, with shifting the emphasis in children's literature from "cautionary instruction to felt experience and adventure" (Stahl, p. 37).

Reader Response

The shift from cautionary instruction to felt experience and adventure—or from didactic to imaginative writing—described by Stahl is congruent with the transactional theory of reader response, the *mutual* interaction of reader and text. "Books need the reader to create the sensory and emotional experiences carried by printed words on a page" (Hancock, p. x). How we interact with a book is dependent on each individual's prior experience and background knowledge. We now understand the validity of individualized reader response to the text which has replaced previous theories which suggest that the reader will unlock the author's intended meaning of the text with the help and guidance of the teacher.

Louise Rosenblatt's reader response theory described in her landmark 1938 publication, *Literature as Exploration*, has dramatically impacted the way we understand the reading process as well as the way we teach with literature. Rosenblatt's theory considers the personal, social, and cultural contexts in which the reader interacts with the text—in a reciprocal relationship which she describes as "the live circuit set up between reader and text" (Rosenblatt, p. 25). It is the reader's past experiences that, when connected to the text, bring the work to life. "In order to share the author's insight, the reader need not have had identical experiences, but he must have experienced some needs, emotions, concepts, some circumstances and relationships, from which he can construct the new situations, emotions, and understandings set forth in the literary work" (Rosenblatt, p. 81).

Rosenblatts's theory, which is grounded in the emotional connectedness of reader and text, was revolutionary. Previous theories considered the reader's personal response to be an obstacle to their understanding of the text and a barrier to accurately determining the author's true intent. However, Rosenblatt understood that, to construct new knowledge, we must associate it with prior knowledge or past experience, as Piaget's work has taught us, and to do so in a social and cultural context, as Vygotsky's work demonstrates.

Fantasy

Unlike fiction, which *could* happen but never did, fantasy depicts characters and situations that could never exist in the real world. Yet, in a well written fantasy novel, the reader willingly suspends their disbelief and relates to the story, in part because of well developed and believable characters, richly described settings, and page-turning plots.

When *Alice's Adventures in Wonderland* was published in 1866 it was considered by many to be the first children's book written for the pure pleasure and entertainment of the reader. Unlike previous *first* children's books that were intended to entertain, *Alice's Adventures in Wonderland* had no dual purpose of instructing children while likewise entertaining them. This high fantasy novel, created by Charles Lutwidge Dodgson under the pen name of Lewis Carroll, was deliberately written with a complete and total absence of didacticism. In fact, Lewis Carroll pokes fun at instructional lessons as evidenced in this passage:

> "And how many hours a day did you do lessons?" said Alice, in a hurry to change the subject.
> "Ten hours the first day," said the Mock Turtle: "Nine the next, and so on."
> "What a curious plan!" exclaimed Alice.
> "That's the reason they're called lessons," the Gryphon remarked: "because they lessen from day to day."
> This was quite a new idea to Alice, and she thought it over a little before she made her next remark.
> "Then the eleventh day must have been a holiday?"
> "Of course it was," said the Mock Turtle.
> "And how did you manage on the twelfth?" Alice went on eagerly.
> "That's enough about lessons," the Gryphon interrupted in a very decided tone. "Tell her something about the games now" (Carroll, L., 1865).

Alice's Adventures in Wonderland contains all of the elements of a high fantasy adventure. After falling asleep, our hero, Alice, crosses the threshold from the real world into the fantasy world, returning to the real world at the end of the story to complete her cyclical journey. She encounters a host of special characters, resolves conflicts, and ingests strange potions which leave the reader wondering whether she fell asleep and/or suffered the hallucination of her colorful escapades, or whether her adventure actually took place.

Given the powerful combination of pun, symbolism, nonsense, and whimsy, it is understandable that Alice has fallen under the heavy hands of scholars who wish to comprehend her true meaning. Whether the critic's interpretation is political, metaphysical, Freudian, allegorical, or psychoanalytical, Carroll's facility with the English language and his brilliant play on words lend a distinct richness to the story and account for its enduring popularity. It's no wonder that literary analysts have felt compelled to unlock her perceived secrets.

Following *Alice's Adventures in Wonderland* and *Through the Looking Glass*, there appeared a host of popular novels written in the high fantasy genre. Often crafted as a trilogy, quartet, or series of continuing quests, some of the most popular and recognizable titles today are *The Chronicles of Narnia* by C. S. Lewis (1951–1956), *The Lord of the Rings Trilogy* by J. R. R. Tolkien (1965), and the *Harry Potter* series by J. K. Rowling (1998–present), further popularized by the movie industry's film versions of these stories.

Novels in the high fantasy genre have found their place among the most compelling and revered literary works of our time. Characters, settings, and plots that capture the young reader's imagination encourage children to visualize possibilities beyond the real world. Based on the universal theme of good v. evil—and carefully constructed to express its internal logic—readers can reflect on their own values and morals while living vicariously through the heroic protagonists in these page turning adventures. These stories tantalize the imagination while revealing inner truths about the human condition, a far cry from the didactic cautionary tales and instructional text that predominated children's books for centuries.

Conclusion

The absence of didacticism however, is not the absence of violence, nor of any number of disturbing situations. On the contrary, real life situations in all their complexity must be presented convincingly in the literature in order for it to resonate with the reader. The content needn't be whitewashed, dumbed-down, or otherwise compromised or glossed over for it to appeal to children, providing it is developmentally appropriate for the targeted audience.

Many popular authors such as Dahl, Rowling, and Snicket routinely place their protagonists in the most dire of circumstances. Most readers can easily relate to the raw human emotion felt by these unfortunate souls, whether the reader has actually endured similar conditions or merely imagined themselves in like circumstances, and it is this reader–text connection that is vital to a satisfying reading experience.

So Heinrich Hoffmann was not the first, nor was he the last author of children's literature to portray children who are the victims of violence, and it is unlikely that the violence alone is what so many find objectionable, but the manner in which the violence is portrayed. While authors such as Heinrich Hoffmann and Hilaire Belloc, who wrote *The Bad Child's Book of Beasts* in 1898, use violence somewhat gratuitously, Rowling and Dahl use it to assist the reader in gaining sympathy for the protagonist and to create a deeper contrast between good and evil.

There are other authors however, who use violence in children's literature in irreverent, whimsical, or humorously repugnant ways, such as Edward Gorey and Shel Silverstein, but these authors and their style of writing is dramatically different than that of Hoffmann's cautionary tales, or Dahl's chapter books, or Rowling's novels. Silverstein's work, in particular his popular poetry collection titled *Where the Sidewalk Ends*, has a mischievous flair that appeals to children who delight in its impudent style. Some parents have objected to its violent content—children are eaten by boa constrictors, for example—but when this violence is presented in the same context as children who belch, pick noses, and have their mouths cemented shut by too many peanut butter sandwiches, most readers understand that the poems are meant to be silly and nonsensical.

Edward Gorey's work, on the other hand, is much darker, even macabre. He creates what some would categorize as violent and disturbing children's stories and poems, but his work is not actually intended for an audience of children. His *Gashleycrumb Tinies* endure the most despicable circumstances. This alphabet book written in 1962 depicts the Tinies from A to Z succumbing to heinous acts of violence. Amy falls down the stairs while Basil is assaulted by bears. Clara wastes away and Desmond is thrown from his sleigh. Each child, depicting the next consecutive letter in the Roman alphabet, succumbs to violence which is at times humorous: Neville dies of ennui, James ingests lye, and Olive is impaled by an awl.

Every good story has a conflict to be resolved—or not—for it is the conflict and how it is handled by and affects the protagonist that captures the reader's attention. Violence is often an integral component of this and fortunately authors have moved away from the superfluous violence of the nineteenth century children's cautionary tales toward a much richer literary tradition wherein the violence, if present at all, is an integral part of the text and is used judiciously to reveal the universal conflict of good v. evil.

Authors who refrain from writing down to children and instead present protagonists who experience realistic life events and believable human emotions, to which readers can make meaningful connections, provide high quality reading material that will surely capture the imaginations of many future generations of young readers.

Illustrations

The following illustrations are from the *English Struwwelpeter*, 60th Edition.

Figure 1. Foreword to the *English Struwwelpeter*, 60th Edition.

Figure 2. Shock-headed Peter.

2. THE STORY OF CRUEL FREDERICK.

Here is cruel Frederick, see!
A horrid wicked boy was he;
He caught the flies, poor little things,
And then tore off their tiny wings,
He kill'd the birds, and broke the chairs
And threw the kitten down the stairs;
And Oh! far worse than all beside,
He whipp'd his Mary, till she cried.

Figure 3.   The Story of Cruel Frederick.

Figure 4.   The Dreadful Story about Harriet and the Matches.

4. THE STORY OF THE INKY BOYS.

As he had often done before,
The woolly-headed black-a-moor
One nice fine summer's day went out
To see the shops and walk about;
And as he found it hot, poor fellow,
He took with him his green umbrella.
Then Edward, little noisy wag,
Ran out and laugh'd, and wav'd his flag;
And William came in jacket trim
And brought his wooden hoop with him;
And Arthur, too, snatch'd up his toys
And join'd the other naughty boys;
So, one and all set up a roar
And laugh'd and hooted more and more,
And kept on singing, — only think! —
"Oh! Blacky, you're as black as ink."

Figure 5.   The Story of the Inky Boys.

Figure 6. The Story of the Man That Went Out Shooting.

Figure 7.   The Story of the Little Suck-a-Thumb.

Figure 8.   The Story of Augustus Who Would Not Have Any Soup.

Figure 9.   The Story of Fidgety Philip.

Figure 10.   The Story of Johnny Head-in-Air.

Figure 11.   The Story of Flying Robert.

This is the end of the *Struwwelpeter* illustrations.

Other Illustrations

Figure 12.   Max and Moritz: A Juvenile History in Seven Tricks.

Figure 13.   Struwelliese.

Bibliography

Aries, P. (1962) *Centuries of Childhood: A Social History of Family Life*. NY: Alfred A. Knopf

Basore, J. W. (1963) *Seneca: Moral Essays*. Cambridge, MA: Cambridge University Press

Blume, J. (1970) *Are You There God? It's Me, Margaret*. NY: Bantam, Doubleday, Dell

Blyton, E. (1949) *Five Get Into Trouble*. UK: Hodder & Stoughton Children's Division

Bogart, D. (Ed.) (2003) *The Bowker Annual: Library and Book Trade Almanac*. (48th Ed.) NJ: Information Today, Inc.

Carroll, L. (1865) *Alice's Adventures in Wonderland*.

Cleverley, J., and Phillips, D. C. (1986) *Visions of Childhood: Influential Models from Locke to Spock*. NY: Teacher's College Press

deMause, L. (Ed.) (1974) *The History of Childhood*. NY: The Psychohistory Press

Elias, N. (1978) *The Civilizing Process: The Development of Manners—Changes in the Code of Conduct and Feeling in Early Modern Times*. Oxford, England: Blackwell Publishers, Ltd.

Galef, D. "You've Got To Be Cruel To Be Kind: The Life of Roald Dahl." *The Lion and the Unicorn*, 20:2 (1996 Dec), pp.272–74

Jacobs, J. S. and Tunnell, M. O. (2004) *Children's Literature, Briefly*. Upper Saddle River, NJ: Pearson Education

Hoffmann, H. (1995) *Slovenly Betsy*. Bedford, MA: Applewood Books

———. (c.1890) *English Struwwelpeter (60th Ed.)* Frankfurt: Literarische Anstalt Rutten & Loening

Hunt, P. (2001) *Children's Literature*. Oxford, England: Blackwell Publishers, Ltd.

Merriam, E. (2002) *Spooky ABC*. NY: Simon & Schuster Books for Young Readers

Metcalf, E. "Civilizing Manners and Mocking Morality: Dr. Heinrich Hoffmann's *Struwwelpeter*." *The Lion and the Unicorn: A Critical Journal of Children's Literature*, 20:2 (1996 Dec), pp. 201–16

Parfrey, A. (1999) *Struwwelpeter. Fearful Stories and Vile Pictures to Instruct Good Little Folks.* CA: Feral House

Power, F. C., Higgins, A., and Kohlberg, L. (1989) *Lawrence Kohlberg's Approach to Moral Education.* NY: Columbia University Press

Savelsberg, J. J. (1996) "*Struwwelpeter* at One Hundred and Fifty: Norms, Controls, and Discipline in the Civilizing Process." *The Lion and the Unicorn: A Critical Journal of Children's Literature*, 20 (1996), pp. 181–200. Johns Hopkins University Press

Sommers, N. (1992) "Between the Drafts," in *College Composition and Communication.* 43 p. 23–31. National Council of Teachers of English

Stedman, R. C., et al. (1976) *Family Life.* Waco, TX: Word Books

Tatar, M. (1987) *The Hard Facts of the Grimms' Fairy Tales.* NJ: Princeton University Press

Taylor, A. (1851) *Original Poems for Infant Minds.* NY: R. Carter and Bros.

Weiss, G. (1996) "Tricky Dick: *Struwwelpeter* and American Politics." *The Lion and The Unicorn* 20, pp. 217–228

Wiedmann, U. (Autumn 2000) "The Inflammable Maiden: Some Remarks on Naughty Girls." *The Princeton University Library Chronicle* 62.1, pp. 72–82

Wortis, J. (1974) *Tricky Dick and His Pals.* Quadrangle/The New York Times Book Co.

Zipes, J. (1999) "Introduction," in *Struwwelpeter: Fearful Stories and Vile Pictures to Instruct Good Little Folks.* CA: Feral House

———. (2000) "The Perverse Delight of Shockheaded Peter." *Theatre* 30:2 (2000) pp. 129–43

———. (2001) *Sticks and Stones: The Troublesome Success of Children's Literature From Slovenly Peter to Harry Potter.* NY: Routledge

Index

Aesop's Fables, 20
Ages of Life, 14–15
Alcott, L. M., 21, 73
Alice in Wonderland, 19, 21, 75–76
amputation, 4, 9, 29, 50
Arabian Nights, 21
Aries, P., 14

Basal Readers, 23
Basore, 16
Beatle-mania, 47
Begbie, E., 60
Belloc, H., 77
Biblia Pauperum, 20
Block, F., 17–18
Blume, J., 12–13
Blyton, E., 12–13
Bogart, D., 11
Brazil, A., 14
Brownell, K., 31
burning girls, 27, 83

Carroll, L., 21, 75
cartoons, 26, 30, 49

cautionary tales, 5, 21, 27; females in,
    63; misdeed and punishment, 43
Centuries of Childhood, 14
chapbooks, 20
character development, 40–41
child: abuse, 8; sacrifice, 16
child development, 5, 7, 11, 26
childhood, 11, 14–15
child rearing practices, 2, 3, 8, 11, 12
children: as evil beings, 11, 15–17, 22;
    selling of, 17
Cleverley, J., 12, 17
cognitive development, 22–23
Comenius, J. A., 71, 73
comprehension strategies, 23, 25–26
contemporary children's literature, 11,
    71
Cotton, J., 20

Dahl, R., 38–42
Darwin, C., 26, 28; racial capitulation
    model, 26
decoding strategies, 25–26
Defoe, D., 21

Dirks, R., 86
deMause, 7, 11, 15–16, 43–44
developmental appropriateness, 4
didacticism, 2, 6, 8, 21–22, 24, 71;
    absence of, 72; Teutonic, 62
Dio Chrysostom, 44
discipline practices, 44–45
disobedience, 7

Egyptian Struwwelpeter, 60
engaged reading, 71
Erikson, E., 22; theory of child
    development, 22–23
etiquette, 15, 46
evil characters: devils, 44; God, 44;
    Jews, 44; witches, 44

fantasy, 6, 19, 75
Freud, S., 26–28

Galef, D., 38
Germanic folk tales, 43
good v. evil, 76, 77
Gorey, E., 77
Grimm: Brothers, 5–6, 20–21; fairy
    tales, 5
Gutenberg, J., 27

Haeckel, E., 26
Hall, G. S., 26
Halloween, 31
Hancock, M., 107
Hitler, 47, 61;
Hitler's Youth, 47
Hlawacek, A., 60
Hoffmann, Heinrich, 1, 3–7, 8–10
Hornbook, 20
humor, 35
Hunt, P., 12

illustrative technique, 47
infantacide, 16–17
Irving, W., 21

Jacobs, J., 71

Katzenjammer Kids, 62, 64
Kinder Und Haus Marchen, 5, 21

Langer, W., 7
Lewis, C. S., 76
literary standards, 23
literature, definition of, 71
Little Red Cowboy Hat, 19
Little Red Riding Hood, 6, 19
Locke, J., 24
Looney Tunes, 24, 30; context, 30;
    enculturation, 34; reason, 33;
    repetition, 32; style, 32
Lowell, S., 19

Mädchenstruwwelpeteriades, 63
Mahler, M., 28
main character, 38–39
marginalized populations, 35
Max and Moritz, 64, 65, 90
McGuffy's Eclectic Primer, 72
Merriam, E., 31
Metcalf, M., 24–25, 45, 48
modern picture books, 24
Montessori, M., 18
Muller, F., 26

Nazi: Germany, 47; ideology, 47; party,
    47, 61
Netolitzky, R., F., and M., 60
Newbery, J., 21, 73
nineteenth century children's literature,
    2, 43
Nixon, R., 61–62

oral story telling, 20
Orbitus Sensualium Pictus, 73

parallel construction, 50–51
Parfrey, A., 37
parody, 59

Payne, L., 16
pedagogy, 24
Perrault, C., 19
Phillips, D. C., 12, 17, 18
Piaget, J., 22, 25, 28, 74; theory of child
    development, 22
Political Struwwelpeter, the, 60
Power, F., 40
Puritans, 17, 22

racism, 45, 62
Reader Response, 19, 20, 74
reading level, 32
Reformation, 44
Rosenblatt, L., 74
Rousseau, J., 18
Rowling, J. K., 40, 77

Sauer, W., 48–50
Savelsberg, J., 44–46
secondary characters, 38–39
Sendak, M., 49
Seneca, 16
Shock Headed Peter, 1, 81
Silverstein, S., 77
Slovenly Betsy, 63
Snicket, L., 40
Sommers, N., 46–47
Soranus of Epheuss, 16
Staake, B., 62–63
stage development theorists, 4
Stahl, J. D., 73–74
St. Augustine, 7

Stedman, R. C., 18
Struwwelpeter: as picture book, 24;
    format, 51; Museum, 59; rhyming
    patterns, 25; stylistic elements, 23
Struwwelhitler, 1, 60–61
Summerhill School, 18

Tatar, M., 6
Taylor, Jane and Ann, 2; Twinkle
    Twinkle Little Star, 2; The Little
    Fisherman, 2
television, 30–32, 34
Thoth the Inky Boy, 60
Tiger Lillies, 1, 43, 62
Tolkein, J. R. R., 76
transactional theory, 74
Tricky Dick and His Pals, 60–62
Twain, M., 73–74
Tunnell, M., 71–72

Vendetta, S., 37
violence, 29–30, 41
vocabulary, 32
Vygotsky, L., 22–23, 74;
theory of child development, 31

Warner, G., 13
Weiss, G., 60
Wesley, J., 17
Wiedmann, U., 27, 63
Wortis, J., 61–62

Zipes, J., 8, 36–37, 43

About the Author

Dr. Barbara Smith Chalou graduated from the University of Massachusetts, Amherst, where she studied folklore and children's literature. She currently teaches a children's literature course at the University of Maine, Presque Isle, and lives in Northern Maine, overlooking the Canadian border, with her husband and their Newfoundland, Annie.